PORTFOLIO

IF YOU DON'T HAVE BIG BREASTS, PUT RIBBONS ON YOUR PIGTAILS

Barbara Corcoran, the founder and chairman of The Corcoran Group, is a motivational dynamo. She lives in New York City with her husband, son, and four stepchildren. For more information about her company, visit www.corcoran.com.

Bruce Littlefield is a journalist and playwright. He recently used Barbara's lessons to open The Rosendale Cement Company, a restaurant in upstate New York.

Praise for Barbara Corcoran and
If You Don't Have Big Breasts,
Put Ribbons on Your Pigtails

"[*If You Don't Have Big Breasts, Put Ribbons on Your Pigtails*] will leave you laughing and crying, but most of all confident that you too can make this world of business work for you."
—Gail Evans, author of *Play Like a Man, Win Like a Woman*

"Ms. Corcoran, a fifty-one-year-old former receptionist who started her current real estate firm with just seven agents in 1978, now commands the kind of market power that makes her smaller competitors tremble with envy."　　　　　　　—*The Wall Street Journal*

"Barbara Corcoran may be New York's real estate diva, but it's her homemaker mother to whom she looks for inspiration."
—*Crain's New York Business*

"Barbara Corcoran is the most quoted, most visible Manhattan real estate agent on the scene today."　　　　—*New York* magazine

"A witty memoir and a powerful guidebook on how to get ahead.... An emotionally charged and intellectually energetic book, which will give people ideas on how to motivate, invigorate and otherwise encourage any group that they lead, and organization they build."
—Bookreporter.com

"Entrepreneurs' visions don't always translate well to the page, but Corcoran's book . . . is cleanly written and humorous. The squeaky-clean Waltons-esque descriptions of Corcoran's family lend it an almost folksy feel." —*Fortune Small Business*

"Her manner is frank and energetic, a team captain who gives total commitment and expects it in return. But for all her drive, she has no airs." —*The New York Times*

"When once a waitress, real estate queen Barbara Corcoran complained to her mum that the ones with the big breasts were the ones getting the big tips. Mama told her: 'So, in the absence of big breasts, wear pigtails and put ribbons on them.' She did, and it worked."
—Cindy Adams, *New York Post*

"In Manhattan, where real estate is not just a major industry but also a full-contact sport, Barbara Corcoran is hall-of-fame material."
—Inc.com

"Mom takes the cake here, but you have to toast Barbara Ann for applying her dictums. The business she's in is almost beside the point: Corcoran could be selling plumbing supplies, and the story would still fly." —*Kirkus Reviews*

"She has interesting stories to tell and many weighty points to make, all presented with flair and humor . . . contains down-to-earth, nitty-gritty advice for succeeding in sales."
—Jack Covert, 800-CEO-READ

"A funny handbook for professional sales savvy—that works . . . a likeable and worthwhile book, an honorable contribution with heart." —*Publishers Weekly*

"A hot entry on the business-book lists, chronicling twenty-eight years worth of the sass, savvy, and street smarts . . . The queen of New York real estate explains how she turned a small business into a multibillion-dollar colossus." —*BusinessWeek* online

"Florence Corcoran's maxims have guided Barbara through slumps, booms, and occasional feuds with the likes of Donald Trump."
—*American Way*

"Corcoran is a lightning bolt of energy caught in a 5-foot-6 frame."
—*USA Today*

"An affirmation of innate feminine common sense and a warm memoir of family life that's too vividly recalled to be saccharin. [*If You Don't Have Big Breasts, Put Ribbons on Your Pigtails*] serves up a generous slice of real life with a scoop of sweet humor on the side."
—*Blue Stone Press*

"Living proof that bad grades and past failures can't be used to predict the future." —*Connecticut Post*

"Corcoran has taken what others consider a liability and turned it into an asset." —*ADDitude*

"As you might expect from such an overachiever, her book, [*If You Don't Have Big Breasts, Put Ribbons on Your Pigtails*], is on the *New York Times* bestseller list." —*Sunday Times* (London)

COMMENTS FROM READERS

"From the minute you open the book, it is funny and thought-provoking. Mixing a funny story that everyone can relate to with practical knowledge and important things you need to know about how to treat other people in the business world made this book awesome to read. . . . I enjoyed every minute of it."
—Tammy Kershner, Lancaster, Pennsylvania

"No matter what business you are in, this book will encourage you to work harder, have more fun and not quit! I had to stay up late to finish it and could turn right around and read it again."
—Kathi Alberson, Las Cruces, New Mexico

"Barbara Corcoran's book is a hilarious account of her successful rise to the top of the New York real estate market. Throughout the book she reflects back on her childhood, citing funny anecdotes and the lessons her mother teaches her to help cope with her challenges. . . . I found myself laughing out loud every time I picked it up."
—Christine Detrick, southern California

"Barbara's book is inspirational, heartwarming and motivational. Women of every walk of life will definitely be connected to Barbara's story of growth and determination. I couldn't put this book down."

—Nancy Ramacitti, USA

"This is not a book about the real estate industry, it's a book about life. EVERYONE will take away something after reading it."

—Linda B., Green Brook, New Jersey

"[*If You Don't Have Big Breasts, Put Ribbons on Your Pigtails*] is like having a personal business coach for a fraction of the price. . . . This book is both highly entertaining and practical, loaded with wonderful stories about growing up in a large family and how those dynamics helped transform a determined young girl into an incredibly successful businesswoman. There's lots of good business advice, plenty of stories that address the proverbial bumps in the road and how she turned obstacles or failures into her advantage."

—Stancy DuHamel, New York, New York

"One of my most treasured books! This book is for everyone. Packed within is priceless information for both the businessperson and non-businessperson alike. Once you start reading this book you won't want to put it down and you won't be the same as when you started it, because you'll feel better about yourself and look at whatever obstacles you have to overcome in a different way."

—Pauline Mucciaccio, Brooklyn, New York

"I picked up this book because I had a friend that worked for The Corcoran Group and it blew me away. I gained such an admiration for Barbara Corcoran and how she founded her empire on such basic, common sense principles, and a lot of hard work!"

—Justin D. Whitney, New York, New York

"Barbara's book is necessary reading for anyone who wants to make their dreams come true! The book is filled with inspiring anecdotal wisdom, and the often unconventional advice from her mom is hilarious"

—Natalie Sykes, Washington, D.C.

"I thought this book was terrific—an entertaining and informative way to apply common sense, imagination, and humor to business situations in a way that works. Should be read by people who want to be successful in ANY field (including parenting). A fast moving, inspiring read that almost everyone will relate to. Also just a thoroughly honest look into the mind of a very successful person."

—Michael O'Reilly, New York, New York

"It grabbed me, pulled me in, and I finished it in two nights. This is not a get rich in real estate book, but a wonderful story of one woman's struggle to the top. . . . The truth is finally out, hard work, dedication, and a fair amount of luck can take you there."

—Stephen J. Barnett, London, Kentucky

"The stories were humorous and educational at the same time. The book's style was unique. I couldn't stop laughing at the funny stories. No one in business or sales should work another day without reading this book." —Gary Gellman, USA

"Full of thoughts and stories that are perfect no matter where you are in your career or what you want to do, even if you are not a 'businessperson.' Barbara's stories are humorous, fun, and make you want to keep reading. The book keeps your interest, even for a person like me who does not consider himself a 'reader' and has a short attention span, I could not put the book down."

—Pete Grover, New York, New York

"You've got to read this book if you have ever dreamed of being powerful and rich and thought it could never happen to you. Here is a girl working in a diner having worked at over twenty different jobs and she ends up being an adversary and acquaintance of Donald Trump. This book is for everyone who wants a better life"

—Paul H. Story, Panama City, Florida

"Fantastic! I couldn't put this book down. Her wit and neverending commitment to perfection shines through in her most recent work. I can't wait to see it on the Big Screen." —Gary Gellman, USA

"How fabulous that out of a little, dinky, blue-collar town would there rise up from the shadows a success story like Barbara's. I read this book nonstop from cover to cover and it was easy reading and fantastic advice." —Donna Bruno, Englewood, New Jersey

"Barbara's success is not based on being in the right place at the right time—far from it—Barbara's success is based on solid business smarts, great people skills, and the ability to stick to her beliefs."
—David Moon, Toronto, Canada

"What a refreshing read for a business book! By using stories and anecdotes Barbara Corcoran does a great job of showing how lessons learned early in life apply to us in our busy, crazy, hectic times of today."
—Joseph T. Higgins, Tucson, Arizona

"You must read this book if you want to grow as a salesperson, businessperson or just as a person. Get it for your kids also, so they know that anything is possible with hard work and creative thinking. It will make you laugh, cry, and dream! It shows that you can start with humble beginnings and conquer the mountaintops. Barbara paved a new path on old worn out streets. She changed the rules for the big boys in Manhattan real estate and now they play by her rules."
—John Rowley, Raleigh, North Carolina

"I own a real estate company in Denver, Colorado, and this book has given me the confidence and tools to make me and my company a success! I credit this book with increasing my sales, giving me the management skills needed to run a company, and the ability to hire the right people. A must have!" —Calley Hughes, Denver, Colorado

"This book made me aware of the importance of instilling a positive self-image in my children. It was absolutely hysterical! The suggestions are priceless and I will implement them in my future endeavors with business and family." —Kristin Dietrich, New Paltz, New York

"Barbara bases her enormous successes on the lessons she learned from her mom—basic lessons, like acknowledging and working with your best characteristics. This book is a must-read for anyone who admires a self-made success. Barbara Corcoran is an inspiration and this book will capture your heart."
—Eleanor Guzzo, Howard Beach, New York

If You Don't Have Big Breasts, Put Ribbons on Your Pigtails

And Other Lessons I Learned from My Mom

Barbara Corcoran
with Bruce Littlefield
Also known as *Use What You've Got*

PORTFOLIO
Published by the Penguin Group
Penguin Group (USA) Inc., 375 Hudson Street,
New York, New York 10014, U.S.A.
Penguin Books Ltd, 80 Strand, London WC2R 0RL, England
Penguin Books Australia Ltd, 250 Camberwell Road, Camberwell,
Victoria 3124, Australia
Penguin Books Canada Ltd, 10 Alcorn Avenue,
Toronto, Ontario, Canada M4V 3B2
Penguin Books India (P) Ltd, 11 Community Centre, Panchsheel Park,
New Delhi – 110 017, India
Penguin Books (N.Z.) Ltd, Cnr Rosedale and Airborne Roads, Albany,
Auckland, New Zealand
Penguin Books (South Africa) (Pty) Ltd, 24 Sturdee Avenue,
Rosebank, Johannesburg 2196, South Africa

Penguin Books Ltd, Registered Offices:
80 Strand, London WC2R ORL, England

First published as *Use What You've Got* in the United States of America by Portfolio,
a member of Penguin Putnam Inc. 2003
Published as *If You Don't Have Big Breasts, Put Ribbons on Your Pigtails*
in paperback 2004

5   7   9   10   8   6

Copyright © Barbara Corcoran and Bruce Littlefield, 2003
All rights reserved

Illustrations by John Segal

THE LIBRARY OF CONGRESS HAS CATALOGED THE HARDCOVER EDITION AS FOLLOWS:
Corcoran, Barbara (Barbara Ann)
Use what you've got : and other business lessons I learned
from my mom / Barbara Corcoran with Bruce Littlefield.
p. cm.
ISBN 1-59184-002-3 (hc.)
ISBN 1-59184-033-3 (pbk.)
1. Corcoran, Barbara (Barbara Ann). 2. Women real estate agents—
United States—Biography. 3. Real estate business—United States.
I. Littlefield, Bruce (Bruce Duanne). II. Title.
HD278.C67 A3 2003
333.33'092—dc21
[B]   2002030838

Printed in the United States of America
Set in Bauer Bodoni

For Mom
(and Dad)

All of the author's profits from this book benefit specialized schools for dyslexic children.

Contents

Introduction
10 Kids, 1 Bath

My mother always says my memory is bigger than my life. Well, here's what I remember.

I grew up beneath a giant cliff on the bottom floor of a three-story house in New Jersey. It was a sliver of a town called Edgewater, and it was two blocks wide and one mile long, just across the Hudson River from Manhattan. My house was easy to find—it was the brown clapboard sitting right below the gigantic *L* of the flickering PALISADES AMUSEMENT PARK sign—and through most of my childhood it was home to twenty-one people.

Uncle Herbie and Aunt Ethel lived on the top floor with their two teen daughters. Nana Henwood lived in the front half of the second floor; the Roanes and their two Peeping Tom sons lived in the back. My family, the Corcorans, lived on the ground floor—the best floor, we thought. We were six girls sharing the middle room we called "the girls' room" and four boys sharing the back room we called "the boys' room." My parents, Florence and Ed, slept on the black vinyl Castro convertible in the living room.

But I never saw my mother sleep. In fact, she only sat down during dinner and later for about three minutes in the tub of our one bathroom. Although Mom was perennially pregnant, she was always on the move—a blurry blue Sears housedress topped by a wavy blond perm and supported by two sturdy speed-walking legs. She had bulging purple varicose veins that grew with each child, and I was always worried that they were going to pop. But they didn't.

On any given day, Mom could be found in one of two places: the outside landing, where she hung the laundry, or the kitchen, where she jogged between the ironing board and the oven. It seemed my mother could do a hundred things at once, all the while keeping at least one of her blue eyes on her ten children.

"Watch yourself, Eddie!" she'd shout down from the landing to my oldest brother in the side yard. "Remember, you're a born leader and all the boys are watching you!" Then she'd vroom down the fourteen wooden steps, hip the laundry basket through the banging screen door into the kitchen, and dump it onto the table.

"You're the absolute *best* helper, Ellen," she'd say as my eager sister did the folding. "You're going to make a *wonderful* mother!"

Shortly after noon, Mom would begin preparations for dinner, served nightly at six o'clock sharp. "Barbara Ann!" she'd yell down the basement stairs as she peeled potatoes. "Come on up here and take Florence, Tommy, and Mary Jean. They need some entertainment and if you're going to be a star, you'll need to practice."

And that was my mother's genius. She kept her house going by putting her finger on the special gift she saw in each of her children, and making each and every one of us believe that that gift was uniquely ours. Whether it was true or not, we all believed it.

It was Nana Henwood who predicted my destiny.

Besides being almost a midget, my grandmother also had the honor of being our bedtime masseuse. While my mother packed our lunches for the next day, Nana would make the rounds and spend a few minutes with each of her ten grandchildren, rubbing our backs and whispering happiness into our ears.

One night when I was eleven, Nana came to my bed and found me crying. Dark hair had suddenly sprouted all over my arms, and I was hiding the two bearded limbs under the covers.

"Let me see your arms," Nana coaxed.

"No," I cried, "they look like Dad's!"

She pulled my arms from beneath the covers and rubbed them. *"Hairy arms!"* She beamed proudly. *"That means you're going to be rich!"*

A few years later, hoping to fulfill Nana's prophecy, I got my first job as a summer playground supervisor. By the time I turned twenty-four, I'd have twenty-two others.

It was my twenty-fourth job that made me rich. How did I get there?

First, I believed Nana's words.

More important, I used what I learned from my mother.

The CORCORAN Family

JOSEPHINE
NANA

FLORENCE
MOM

EDWIN JR.
DAD

DENISE
DENISE
THE BEAST

BARBARA
BOOGIE BOOGIE
BARBARA

EDWIN III
EDDIE
SPAGHETTI

ELLEN
ELLEN
WATERMELON

JOHN
JUMP JOHNNY
JUMP

THOMAS
TIPPY
TOE TOMMY

MARY JEAN
MARY JEAN
THE BEAN

MARTIN
MARTY
JOE

JEANINE
JEANINE
THE QUEEN

FLORENCE
FRED

BUDDY

PRINCE I

PRINCE II

ZHA-ZHA

SAM

If You Don't Have Big Breasts, Put Ribbons on Your Pigtails

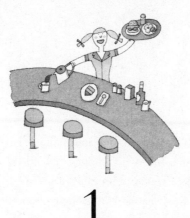

1

If You Don't Have Big Breasts, Put Ribbons on Your Pigtails

The story of my billion-dollar business starts like this: I borrowed a thousand dollars from a friend. Okay, I didn't borrow it. He gave it to me. And he wasn't a friend. He was a boyfriend. But when I moved into my first apartment on East Eighty-sixth Street with two roommates, I did have a thousand dollars to start a real estate company.

It seemed so simple. There'd be virtually no overhead! I'd probably rent two, maybe even three, apartments a day, and we'd be running at a profit by the second Sunday of every month. "All the rest will be gravy," I told my business partner/boyfriend, Ramòne Simòne. "And we'll share the gravy evenly," he added. Or *almost evenly*—49 percent for me and 51 percent for him. After all, he explained, he was the one risking the money.

I was wiping the counter of the Fort Lee Diner the first time Ramòne walked in. It was a quiet night. There were only a few customers in the diner, and the other waitress, Gloria, had them all.

Well, Gloria and her two well-rounded friends. Gloria was built like Dolly Parton with a big bleached-blond swirl of cotton candy hair. Her breasts were the specialty of the house and had the power to lure men off the street, even if they weren't hungry. She could carry six cups of coffee stacked on top of them, and never spill a drop.

Gloria and her dynamic duo had put the Fort Lee Diner on the map, and watching the twins bounce around the diner had become sport in Fort Lee. I was watching her work the front section and, in an effort to feel busy, I was wiping the barren Formica landscape in front of me with a soggy white rag.

The double aluminum doors at the far end of the diner opened and in walked my destiny. I knew he was there before I ever looked up. With his dark skin and jet-black hair, he was unlike the working-class customers who frequented the place. In his blue aviator shades, he was different, probably from a land very far away. At least across the river, I figured.

I had seen his crisp, white flat collar and rich dark suit on only one other person in my twenty-one years—Irvin Rosenthal, the elderly owner of the Palisades Amusement Park. The Park hovered atop the cliff above our house like a blinking, flashing, whirring spaceship. During the summers of my childhood, when Mr. Rosenthal drove down Undercliff Avenue in his black limousine, all the kids of Edgewater ran up to his car like chickens to the feet of a farmer's wife, each of us hoping to get more than our fair share of free ride tickets. In his finery, Mr. Rosenthal was like a king. We all knew he was rich. Besides the fact that he owned the amusement park, he just smelled different from all of us river rats.

Ramòne smelled different, too, I decided, even from across the room and over the thick aroma of frying bacon and eggs. Instead of asking to sit in Gloria's station, he looked at the manager and, with a quick lift of his chin, pointed toward me, the young innocent behind the counter. He walked across the diner, strutting like a pigeon. My eyes met his blue aviator shades. *Finally*, I thought, as he took a seat at the second stool, *an interesting customer*.

He ordered a cup of tea, and while I banged in and out of the swinging kitchen door, he sat and sipped it, hardly moving, just watching as I worked my counter.

I loved my counter. It was my territory, and everything that went on there was under my control. There were nine stools and every third one had a setup: glass sugar container, ketchup bottle, salt and pepper shakers, and a tin filled with white napkins. Since I was stuck behind the counter face-to-face with my customers, I often served as their dinner companion. So I made the most of it and entertained them with conversation.

Ramòne told me he was from the "Basque Country." I didn't know if Basque was a town in New Jersey or not, and I suppose my face gave me away. It wasn't just any place in Spain, he explained, it was the upper echelon of French-Spanish society.

He said his father had blond hair and blue eyes, just like mine, and he liked the red ribbons on my pigtails. I smiled, spritzing the napkin tins and chrome tops of the sugar containers with Windex and shining them with a paper towel.

He left sixty-five cents on the counter and offered me a ride home. I didn't need to weigh the options—walk the five blocks to the number 8 Lemoine Avenue bus or be driven home by the man from the Basque Country. "I'm finished at ten," I blurted.

After my shift, I took the diner's concrete steps two at a time. Ramòne was parked at the bottom in a buttercup-yellow Lincoln Continental, the kind with the hump on the back. I opened the door and climbed into a car very different from any I'd ever been in. The seats felt like talcum powder against my arms and smelled expensive, unlike the crunchy seats of Dad's blue station wagon.

Ten minutes later, we pulled up to the curb in front of my house. Ray—he said I could call him Ray—followed me up our front steps and into the living room. I offered him a seat on the black vinyl sofa where my parents slept and he was quickly surrounded by a blur of ten blond-haired, blue-eyed cookie-cutter kids. I introduced Ramòne Simòne, from the Basque Country, to my family.

My family hated Ray on sight, especially my mom, who, contrary to her normally welcoming ways, wanted the Dark Knight out of her house as quickly as possible. "He's much older than you" is all I remember her saying after Ray left. What she didn't say screamed loudly in the silence.

Ray waited outside the diner every night and gave me a ride home. I guess you could say we were dating, though I didn't think of the rides that way. He told me he was a big real estate developer and built houses in every town in New Jersey except mine. I also learned that he was fifteen years older than I and was divorced with three daughters. To me, this all added to the intrigue.

A few months later, Ray said a smart girl like me should be living in the Big City, and to get me started, he offered to pay for a week at the Barbizon Hotel for Women. To my mother's dismay, I jumped at his offer and packed up a few belongings.

I carried my suitcase down from the third floor. I had packed only my black ribbed sweater, two pleated skirts, my navy-blue peacoat, and my new pair of pajamas. Mom was standing next to the living room radiator sorting socks.

"Now, Barbara," she said, pushing my bangs away from my eyes and looking out the front door toward the street. "Don't you be fooled by that fancy car!"

"I know, I know, Mom," I said, giving her a quick peck on the cheek and a one-armed hug.

"And remember, if you change your mind, you can always come home."

With that, I hurried down the steps and climbed into Ray's big Lincoln with the yellow leather seats. I felt the same mixture of fear and excitement I did every time the Cyclone clicked toward the top of the big hill. I didn't say a word as Ray revved the car's engine and turned onto Hilliard Avenue, but I did take one last look back at the house sitting beneath the *L* of the Palisades Amusement Park sign.

Ray gave me some money to go buy myself a "real New York outfit." I bought a purple one—a stretchy lavender lace top, lavender corduroy bellbottoms with six lavender buttons on the hip, and a pair of lace-up, knee-high, lavender suede boots. I walked out of Bloomingdale's all purple and paraded up Lexington Avenue singing, *"Hey there! Georgy Girl, swinging down the street so fancy free . . ."* I knew I was lookin' good and needed only two more things to stay in New York: a job and an apartment.

The next morning, I put on my new outfit and applied for a receptionist's position with the Giffuni Brothers company on Eighty-third and First. Thelma, my interviewer, explained that the Giffuni Brothers were two wealthy landlords who owned a dozen apartment buildings in Manhattan and Brooklyn. She said I'd be in charge of greeting every tenant who called with: "Good morning, Giffuni Brothers."

By the end of the day, I had landed the receptionist's position and by the end of the week I had used the *Village Voice* want ads to find an apartment three blocks away from the office and two girls to share the rent. I moved myself out of the Barbizon Hotel.

My Giffuni Brothers stint introduced me to Manhattan real estate. I wore my purple outfit eight days a week and probably said, "Good morning, Giffuni Brothers" eight hundred times a day. But after a few months of "Good morning, Giffuni Brothers," I eagerly gave Ray my "no overhead" spiel about running at a profit by the second Sunday of every month, and he gave me the $1,000 to start a real estate company. We became partners and named it Corcoran-Simone. My old boss, Joseph Giffuni, said if I could find a tenant for one of his apartments, he'd pay me a whole month's rent as a commission. He showed me the list of apartments they had for rent, and I picked Apartment 3K, the cheapest one-bedroom on the list.

I created my makeshift Corcoran-Simone office on the sofa one of my roommates had borrowed from her parents. My newly installed pink Princess phone sat silent on the double-tiered mahogany end table, as I stared bleary-eyed at the Sunday *New York Times* classified section. According to my count, there were exactly 1,246 one-bedroom apartments advertised. The ads were five or six lines long and the apartments were all priced between $320 and $380 a month. I noticed the best ads among the lot were the splashy ones with the bigger, bolder headlines like: "FABULOUS 3!" "RIV VU 1 BR." "TRIPLE MINT!!!" followed by a long list of superlatives.

I worked out the numbers on my steno pad, and realized that the big ads were a lot bigger than my budget. I decided to keep my ad to four lines or less in order to make Ray's $1,000 last a whole month. *But how*, I wondered, *could I make my little ad stand out among the biggies and how was I going to draw someone's eye?*

Stretching my neck and looking up from the paper, I thought about my job at the Fort Lee Diner. *Ah, Gloria! Now she had a gimmick.* On my first day at the diner, I saw Gloria had assets I'd never have, and that night went home to fret to my mother: "And when we weren't busy, Mom, my counter was plain empty. Even when Gloria's station was completely filled, men were *still* asking to sit with Gloria and not me."

"Barbara Ann, you've got a great personality," Mom said, as she balanced Baby Florence on her hip and hung a sheet on the line. "You're going to have to learn to use what you've got. Since you don't have big breasts, why don't you tie some ribbons on your pigtails and just be as sweet as you are."

And that's how Ray found me two years later, wearing ribbons on my pigtails and offering a cheerful alternative to the big-breasted, tiny-waisted, blond-bombshell Fort Lee sensation. I considered it a personal victory when a customer walked into the diner and asked to sit with "Pigtails." The simple gimmick pulled them to my counter and my sweet-talking kept them coming back.

Sitting alone in my apartment with the *New York Times* spread open on my lap, I thought about Mom's advice for competing with Gloria's superlatives, and I knew I needed an attention-grabber for Apartment 3K. *How*, I asked myself, *can I put ribbons on a typical one-bedroom in four lines or less and make it stand out from the other 1,246 apartments?*

I took a deep breath and picked up my pink Princess phone. "Hello, Mr. Giffuni," I began. "I've been thinking about your one-bedroom on the third floor, and I think I have a way to rent it for twenty dollars more each month." I had his attention. I told him how Apartment 3K's living room was like every other living room in every other apartment in every other building in New York and convinced him that if he put up a wall separating the living room from the dining alcove, he'd really have something different! Mr. Giffuni hesitated, giving it some thought, and then said he'd have the wall installed that week. I phoned my ad into the paper.

The following Sunday, my first four-line ad (**bold** print counted for two lines) appeared in the *New York Times*:

> **1 BR + DEN $340**
> Barbara Corcoran,
> 212-355-3550

It wasn't a big ad like the others, but it sure offered something more. Why would *anyone* settle for a one-bedroom, when for the same price you could get a one-bedroom with a den?

That Sunday, the calls began. And on Monday I rented my first apartment.

*

MOM'S LESSON #1: If you don't have big breasts, put ribbons on your pigtails.

*

THE LESSON LEARNED
ABOUT USING WHAT YOU'VE GOT

I didn't have a big chest, but I did have a nice personality, a great smile, and the gift of gab. All I needed was my mother's cue to begin using them to my advantage. That was my first lesson in sales.

Although the apartment I advertised wasn't any bigger than the hundreds of others advertised that Sunday, my ad caught attention because it offered something extra—one more room. My "1 BR + DEN" ad enabled the customer to focus on the *perceived* benefit of more space, and the overwhelming response to the ad gave me a lot more bang for my advertising buck.

Good salesmanship is nothing more than maximizing the positive and minimizing the negative. Although your competition might offer something you can't match, that doesn't matter. What matters is that you identify and play up what you've got.

2

Paint the Rocks White and the
Whole Yard Will Look Lovely

October 1973. New York City.

I held the commission check in my hand. *Three hundred and forty dollars!* I was standing on the corner of Eighty-third and First with the check and Mr. Giffuni's list of eleven new apartments for rent. It was October 17, New York was already turning cold, and the navy-blue peacoat I had brought from New Jersey looked just like a navy-blue peacoat I had brought from New Jersey. "I'm going to take this money and buy myself the best coat in New York," I told myself triumphantly.

I held up my check again as if it weren't real and looked at the number: $340.00! I'd seen only one check that was bigger in my entire life, during my dad's one short stint in his own business.

1959. Edgewater, New Jersey.

One Monday night, Dad came to the dinner table and announced, "I'm happy to tell you kids that today I quit my job, and I'm starting my *own* business!" Dad looked really excited. "I won't be working for Mr. Stein as his press foreman anymore!" he continued. "And I'm naming my company 'Pre-Press Preparations.'"

We all listened as Dad laid out his business plan, ten wide-eyed kids and one very wide-eyed mother.

"From now on I'll be known as 'Edwin W. Corcoran, the *president* of Pre-Press Preparations,'" Dad continued. "And I'll also be the company's one-man sales force, but I'll use a pseudo-name for calling my customers." Ellen asked what a "sudo-name" was, and Dad demonstrated with a would-be sales call: "Hello there. This is Paul Peterson of Pre-Press Preparations calling. . . ." I could see red blotches begin to form in the *V* of Mom's blue housedress, a well-known warning signal in our house.

Dad explained how his new company would design and make cardboard boxes. He picked up the Mueller Dairies milk carton from the table, and said, "For instance, if Mr. Mueller hired me, I would decide how big his carton should be, I'd pick the colors, and I'd even draw the cows! I'd also find the right factory to make the cartons. Yep, I'd do it all!"

Within the week, Paul Peterson sold his first client on a job to design a belt buckle box, and President Edwin W. Corcoran asked my brother Tommy and me to sit at his new drafting table and draw buckle designs with his new black Enco drafting pen. We drew six different belt buckles, Dad cut them out, rubber-cemented them onto his white cardboard box prototype, and sent them to press.

The following week, Dad came to the dinner table and we bowed our heads as he recited our usual prayer much faster than usual: "Bless us, Our Lord, for these our gifts which we are about to receive from thy bounty through Christ Our Lord. Amen."

"Amen!" we agreed, and raised our heads to find Dad majesti-
cally holding up a small blue paper in both hands, the same way Father Galloway held his golden chalice on Sundays. Then, with great
fanfare, Dad passed the blue paper around the table.

Each of us stared in awe at what appeared to be a check with a
lot of zeros following the number 1. It was Marty Joe who figured it
out first.

"Why, it's a *thousand dollars!*" he said.

"Yup! That's right, kids!" Dad proclaimed. "We're *RICH*! And
we're *GOING ON VACATION*!!!"

The next morning, my mother packed ten kids, ten bathing
suits, and ten tuna fish on Wonder Breads into our blue station
wagon, and we headed to Asbury Park. Our family had never stayed
in a real hotel, and our stay at the Brighton Beach Hotel proved to be
the most exciting week of our entire childhood.

One month later, Paul Peterson had been let go, Edwin W. Corcoran was out of business, and we were eating on credit at Bubsy's
Grocery Store.

I looked down at my first commission check and pondered, *Should I
take the money and splurge on a new coat, or shouldn't I?* Remem-
bering that my dad's first check as his own boss had been his last and
that it had taken him ten months to find a new job as a press foreman,
I decided I'd better not. I stuffed the check and the apartment list in
my bag, and headed up the three blocks to my apartment.

As I walked through the lobby, the building's super was perched at
his usual post next to the mailboxes. "Good morning, Mr. O'Rourke," I
chirped as I breezed past the potbellied, red-faced, nosy Irishman. Seeing him always made me think that he must be related to Maggie
O'Shay from Edgewater. Mr. O'Rourke rightfully boasted of running
"the cleanest building in all New York," just as Mrs. O'Shay claimed to
"keep the cleanest house in Edgewater."

1957. Edgewater.

Although there wasn't a garden club in Edgewater, Mrs. O'Shay acted as its self-appointed president. She paced up and down Under-cliff Avenue inspecting each house while doling out her neighbors' secrets as though they were hers to give.

Mrs. O'Shay watched with raised eyebrows as my mother tried time and again to spruce up our yard, and time and time again met only with failure. One spring, Mom laboriously stacked the yard's rocks to form a retaining wall, only to find it slowly eroding when we kids used the larger rocks as roast beefs in our pretend grocery store.

Next, she planted grass, only to learn grass doesn't grow very well on a rock-strewn hill shaded by a giant oak tree. The following spring, Mom dug thirty-six holes to plant a gladiolus garden. She dusted the bulbs with bonemeal and placed each one carefully in its nest. The next morning, the gladiolus bulbs lay waiting by their holes as though they had never been planted. After Mom's roll call yielded nothing but frustrating Not me's, Prince, our collie-wolf-Chihuahua mix, was found guilty of digging for bones.

With stubborn determination, my mother dug thirty-six new holes and spent all of June watering, weeding, and waiting. Finally, one hot day in July, the green stalks began to unfurl their hot-pink, yellow, and bright orange petals. It was the same day Mom came home from the hospital with our new baby sister, Jeanine. Timmy Tom, the skinny five-year-old Harrison kid, stood at our kitchen screen door with a huge bouquet of nearly opened gladiolus. "These are for you and your new baby, Mrs. Corcoran," he said as he handed my mother the three months of work he had plucked from her yard.

Timmy Tom's flower delivery sent my mother right over the edge and down to the Edgewater hardware store. She came home with a gallon of Sherwin-Williams paint and a new idea. She got out her yellow Fuller scrub brush and a bucket of water and called us into the side yard. We spent the afternoon scrubbing the roast-beef-size rocks, while Mom followed behind us with her can of semigloss white. That night, we all pressed our faces to the side yard window to admire our rocks. They glistened brighter than our backyard fireflies.

The next morning, during her usual inspection up and down Undercliff Avenue, Mrs. O'Shay screeched to a halt in front of our house. "Oh! What a lovely yard you have, Mrs. Corcoran!" she exclaimed, admiring the ordinary rocks turned extraordinary. "What a truly lovely yard!" My mother smiled and waved proudly from the front steps, and a Corcoran tradition was born. Each spring thereafter, Mom would gather her children, her can of semigloss white, and her Fuller scrub brush, and we'd spend the day swabbing a fresh coat of paint on the rocks in our truly lovely yard.

I stepped into my apartment and thought about the Giffuni Brothers' check burning a hole in my purse. *Should I buy a new coat or shouldn't I?* I looked down at my lavender Georgy Girl outfit; it had walked down the street so many times it no longer looked fancy free. *Should I or shouldn't I?* Well, I decided, if Mom could cover her old rocks with a coat of white paint, I could certainly cover *my* old outfit with a new coat!

I high-tailed it down to First National City Bank on Fifty-seventh and Park, cashed my Giffuni Brothers check, made a beeline to Fifth Avenue, and marched straight through the grand stone archway of Bergdorf Goodman. I was going to buy myself the *best* coat in the *best* store on the *best* block in all New York!

I asked the red suited doorman where I could find ladies' coats and took the gold-paneled elevator to the second floor. The elevator dinged open, and I tripped into a full city block of coats. A well-clad, matronly saleswoman offered her help, but I was too intimidated to accept her offer and thought of a really original response: "No, thanks, I'm just looking." I puffed up my chest and dove into the sea of coats.

Suddenly, I spotted her from across the room. She was the flashiest one in the whole place. There was nothing plain about her. She had curly brown-and-white fur around a high mandarin collar and a pair of matching cuffs. Her wool was thick, laid in an oversized brown-and-white herringbone pattern. Down her front she had at least a dozen diamond-shaped buttons chiseled out of what looked like bone. Each bone button hooked through its own handmade loop. Her huge shoulder pads rode high and her hem swung low, almost touching the polished wood floor. Everything about her screamed, "HERE I AM!" And for $319 plus tax, she was mine.

My new coat became my signature piece and I never took it off. In it, I not only looked successful, I also *felt* successful. My curious customers asked me what kind of fur it was, and since I'd never spoken to the saleslady, I had no idea. "It looks a lot like my old dog, Prince," I'd joke. For the next two years, I marched in and out of buildings up and down Manhattan wearing my expensive coat and new image for all they were worth.

✳

MOM'S LESSON #2: Paint the rocks white and the whole yard will look lovely.

✳

THE LESSON LEARNED
ABOUT DRESSING THE PART

In business, I've learned that people really *do* judge a book by its cover. When my mother painted her rocks white, everyone bought into the fact that our yard was indeed beautiful. And I've applied the same principle in my business time and again.

By dressing the part of someone successful, I was forced to measure up to my own new image. Whether or not my customers agreed with my taste, at least I looked successful enough to afford a Bergdorf coat. In it, I felt ready to take on the world. And so I did.

In business, I believe the best money spent is on things that create the image of success. I copied the typeface of the famous Tiffany store to make my first business cards and chose a gray ink (no extra charge) instead of the usual black. I rented a pink Princess Trimline phone (one dollar extra per month) because when I picked up the phone, it made me feel just like a big business lady. When my Georgy Girl pants got too tired of walking, I slit the seams, used them as a pattern, and made myself three new pairs of well-cut gabardine trousers (six yards of fabric only forty dollars).

Decked out in my fancy new coat and my French-cut trousers, I offered my customers an elegant business card, feeling like the queen of New York real estate.

Painting the rocks white was my first introduction to the surprising truth that *perception creates reality*. Most people think it's the other way around.

3

If the Sofa Is Ripped, Cover It with Laughter

One month later, on a cold day in November, I arrived home to find a white envelope stuffed under our apartment door.

I opened it and read:

N.Y.C. DEPARTMENT OF HOUSING
NOTICE

11-12-73

FOR: Barbara Corcoran, **Tenant**
FROM: Campagna Holding Corp., **Landlord**
RE: **Premises known as** 345 East 86th Street
       Apartment 9F
       City of New York, New York 10028

NOTICE IS HEREBY GIVEN under the provisions of Chapter 186, section 12 of New York Laws, and those claiming under you to deliver up and quit the premises you presently hold as the tenant of <u>Campagna Real Estate </u>(known as landlord) no later than <u>11-30-1973</u>. **Failing such vacating, legal action shall be commenced to evict you.**

"*. . . legal action shall be commenced to evict you?*" I reread aloud. "Evict *me?*" I stammered into the elevator, clutching the notice in my hand. I went downstairs and found Mr. O'Rourke next to the mailboxes. "Mr. O'Rourke," I sputtered, "I just found this notice under my door and it doesn't make any sense! I know my rent is paid! I always collect it from Jackie and Sandi and send the checks in myself *before* the first of the month. I'm *never* late. Is this some kind of mistake?" I waited for his response, clutching the notice even tighter.

"You'll best be talkin' to the landlord," was all Mr. O'Rourke would say.

I arrived at 9:30 A.M. and walked into the white brick office building at 770 Lexington Avenue. A dusty and elderly secretary reluctantly showed me into my landlord's office. It was decorated in a mix of red velvet and the darkest, shiniest wood I had ever seen. Mr. Campagna was young and shockingly handsome, and I watched him take note of my impressive coat. He offered to take it. I was nervous and felt stronger in my power coat, so I said that I was cold and I'd prefer to leave it on. He offered me a seat.

I sank into the red leather chair and started immediately: "I'm sure there must be some mistake, Mr. Campagna, because I received this eviction notice and I *know* my rent is paid. You see, I always collect the rent from my two roommates by the twenty-fifth of every month and enclose their two checks with mine in the rent envelope and mail it never a day later than the twenty-sixth of the month. It must arrive at your office on either the twenty-seventh or twenty-eighth, I'm sure never later than the twenty-eighth." He sat tapping a pen on his black leather desk pad, returning absolutely no expression, so I kept talking. "Mr. Campagna, we never play loud music, and never ever leave food around. We've never had roaches—not even one."

Mr. Campagna shifted slightly in his chair, but still said nothing, and I felt I was wrestling with air.

I talked faster. "I've never, ever done anything wrong in my life, and would consider myself a fine tenant in every way. I'm proud to be a tenant in your very fine building, Mr. Campagna." No reaction. "Mr. O'Rourke tells me you and your fine wife and your two fine sons also live in your very fine building." As I stumbled through these last fine words, I realized my mandarin fur collar had overtaken my nose and was interfering with my speech. I took a quick look left, then right, and saw that my shoulder pads had been inching up and were now level with my ears. Mr. Campagna sat quietly, staring at a fast-talking blond tuft of hair and two desperate blue eyes.

Finally, he spoke. "You have had a lot of traffic coming in and out of your apartment, Miss Corcoran, both during the day and evening hours." I agreed that I had a lot of customers, and said that my business relied on word of mouth. I added that I was new at it and hoped to have a lot more customers in the future. He looked shocked, shocked to the point of horror.

"You're dressed rather *sophisticated* for such a young girl," he said, examining the bone buttons of my coat and fidgeting with his pen.

And then it hit me.

"Mr. Campagna!" I exclaimed, my mouth wide open in disbelief. "You. Think. I'm. A PROSTITUTE?!"

He said nothing.

"If you knew my mother and knew how I was raised," I told him. "Why, Mr. Campagna, I'm almost a nun!"

Dinnertime. Edgewater.

Dinner at our house was an event—an event we were required to attend. Daily at six o'clock sharp, we gathered around the plywood-covered table, which grew larger with every new child, and took our usual seats. I sat at the foot of the table near the bathroom, though I thought of it as the head. Mom was to my left and between us was Jeanine's high chair.

Tonight, like every night, Mom went around the table asking each child, "And how was your day today?" Mom always circled the table clockwise, starting with Ellen and ending with me.

"And how was *your* day today?" Mom asked Denise, who was sulking over her dinner. "You look worried. Is there anything wrong?"

"Nothing," she answered.

Nothing was not an answer at my mother's table. We all stared at Denise, knowing Mom wasn't moving on until Denise reported something about her day. "My new boyfriend is coming to the house later tonight," Denise blurted.

"Why, that's lovely," Mom responded. "Will he be coming soon? We certainly have enough spaghetti for him. What's the boy's name?"

"Bruce," Denise declared. "And he's rich and he's going to see that we're not."

We all slurped our spaghetti in silence.

"He's going to come and see our house," Denise kept on, "and *see* that we're poor—see that all of us kids sleep in two bedrooms and you and Dad sleep on the living room sofa. And that the sofa is all torn—"

"Stop it! Stop it right there, Denise!" Mom demanded, as she spoon-fed Baby Florence. "*I* won't have any of that talk around this table. We're not poor at all. In fact, *I* think we're rich. It's all in how you look at things. Nana says that if life gives you lemons, make lemonade. And we've got lots of lemonade around here!"

"Lemonade?" Denise sniffled, as the rest of us finished our dinners.

"Yes, lemonade," Mom confirmed, looking around the table. "Are any of you ever hungry?" We all shook our heads no. "And don't you have good clothes on your back?" We all looked down, not sure.

"Well"—Mom smiled—"you don't walk around naked, do you?"

"Barbara does in the back of Charlie's boat," Ellen chimed in.

"Do not."

"Do too."

"What matters," Mom interrupted, "is that if you look at what we've got, I say we've got a lot. We have each other. We laugh together, play together, help each other. We're rich."

"But, *Mom*," Denise cried as if it were her one and only chance for a boyfriend in her whole life, "Bruce is *really* good-looking and he dresses real nice. He's going to walk in and see all the tape holding our sofas together."

Then Mom's face lit up with the birth of an idea. "After dinner," she announced, "we're all making lemonade. Let's finish up, Ellen and Eddie clear the table, and everyone report to the living room."

We gulped our dinner down and quickly finished our after-dinner duties, eager to see how Mom would make lemonade in the living room. "Sometimes," Mom instructed as she strategically sat each of her children on and in front of the two sofas, hiding the duct-taped rips, "things are better than they seem. All you have to do is see them that way! So, see us as *RICH*—and don't move! Don't move a muscle." Our arms and our legs were crisscrossed over one another in a homespun game of Twister. The laughter became contagious. Mom had turned our ripped sofa into a giggling work of art.

When Denise welcomed her boyfriend Bruce into our living room, he didn't notice the rips on the sofas because they didn't matter. What he saw instead was a family that he instantly liked. A family rich with the excitement of being a family.

Mom was right, I thought, looking at the reflection of my furry coat in the polished mahogany of Mr. Campagna's desk. *It's all in how you look at things*.

"Mr. Campagna!" I stated clearly. "I'm *not* a prostitute, I'm a *real estate broker!*"

Mr. Campagna put down his pen and hinted at a smile. "Well, then, Miss Corcoran," he said, "why don't you just tell me how you're finding the real estate market?" I thought he might be testing me, so I told him about the success I was having at Mr. Giffuni's building just three blocks away from his building. It was, of course, the only success I knew. When I told him I had gotten Mr. Giffuni $340 for his third-floor one-bedroom (not mentioning my wall idea), he seemed even more shocked than if I had been a prostitute.

I asked Mr. Campagna who rented *his* apartments, and he made it quite clear that "Mr. Herbert Cramer has always been the *exclusive* agent for *all* the Campagna Properties." After he explained to me what an exclusive was and that it had a "guaranteed commission upon closing," I decided I had better try to get a few of those.

"Mr. Campagna," I asked, "if Mr. Cramer rents all your properties, why are there so many apartments vacant in your building?" He didn't seem to have an answer, so I suggested he give me just one of those apartments to rent. Then, not wanting to appear too pushy, I added, "The one Mr. Cramer likes the least."

Apartment 3C was next door to the superintendent's apartment and had been vacant for a long time. It had a narrow galley kitchen, and a long, straight living room, with no hopes of ever having a den. Apartment 3C faced the back and never saw the light of day. The building at Eighty-sixth Street and First Avenue was in the wrong location. It was just one block too east and just one block too west, and the Gristede's grocery store directly across the street had tons of garbage stacked outside.

I arranged to meet my customers two blocks away on tony East End Avenue so I could begin each showing by admiring the wonderful prewar buildings that lined that avenue. "We're walking toward Fifth Avenue," I'd say as we crossed First Avenue on East Eighty-sixth Street. I'd gesture toward the Gristede's grocery store "so conveniently located right across the street," and then whirl us through the revolving doors into Mr. O'Rourke's "meticulously kept lobby." There I'd find Mr. O'Rourke (my new best salesman) proudly standing next to the mailboxes, and I'd introduce him to our prospective tenants.

He'd turn on his Irish charm and proudly tour them through his spotless service areas and stairwells. I'd thank Mr. O'Rourke and ride my customers up in the elevator, remarking that "the owner is so proud of this building that he moved his own family in."

Once my customers saw all the good things Mr. Campagna's building had to offer, they were writing their checks before I even turned the key of Apartment 3C, Apartment 7F, Apartment 21A. . . .

That's how it came to be that Mr. Herbert Cramer no longer held the exclusive on Mr. Campagna's building.

✳

MOM'S LESSON #3: If the sofa is ripped, cover it with laughter.

✳

THE LESSON LEARNED ABOUT FINDING THE GOOD IN SOMETHING BAD

When Denise whined about the torn sofa, my mother was savvy enough to see the liability as an opportunity and used it to teach us how truly rich we were.

If I hadn't almost been evicted as a prostitute, I wouldn't have had the opportunity to meet my landlord, ask for his listings, and leave with a new apartment to rent. The eviction notice and its happy ending taught me that opportunity hides in the worst situations, when the timing's not right, and when everyone else agrees that the only prudent move is to lie low. Finding opportunity is a matter of believing it's there.

4

Use Your Imagination
to Fill In the Blanks

1975. New York City.

"**Y**ou want to *buy?*" I asked in disbelief as my new customer and I left the Drake Hotel in the backseat of a Yellow Cab. "*Buy* an apartment? Are you sure you don't want to *rent?*" My customer was hot-to-trot. He was heading back to St. Louis the next day and wanted to do so having bought a New York City apartment. I glanced down at the long, neatly typed list of rentals I had planned on showing him and knew I had to fill in the blanks fast.

"No problem," I said as we crossed Lexington Avenue, "no problem at all." I hadn't the faintest idea of how to *sell* apartments, but I knew if I let him out of the cab, he'd be sure to call another broker. "Today is a day of education," I began, pointing out the window. "We'll take a complete tour of *every* neighborhood in Manhattan. You'll learn what each has to offer, and I'll tell you everything good about them as well as everything bad." I figured that would kill four hours. "It's important that you see each neighborhood with an unbiased eye, so today we'll not discuss prices." I said a quick prayer that the *New York Times* classifieds would at least give me a handle on what apartments were selling for. "Once you've seen what's out there, we'll find a quiet place to sit, and you can ask whatever questions you might still have. If we're lucky, we'll have time to squeeze in a bite to eat." I'd walk him to the Yorkville Diner and order the made-from-scratch souvlaki special, I figured, which should swallow another hour to an hour and a half. If my math was correct, I would drop him back at the Drake around four, too late in the day for him to take off with another broker.

"Tomorrow," I continued, "we'll start out bright and early and look at every apartment for sale in the neighborhoods you've selected. I'm sure you'll find that after today's tour, you will see them with a very different, more knowledgeable eye."

I had him in a New York minute. He nodded in dumbfounded agreement.

My buyer never doubted that I knew what I was talking about because although I didn't know the sales market, I knew how to fill in the blanks. It was a talent Mom taught me to recognize one night after dinner in second grade, the day Sister Stella Marie told me I was stupid.

Second grade. Edgewater.

The night Sister Stella Marie ruined my day, I was painfully quiet, while Mom rounded the table asking her usual "And how was your day?" question. Jump Johnny Jump announced that there was a new "cool" kid in the neighborhood and Tippy Toe Tommy reported that he had found a pair of high heels in the Mertzes' trash. When Mom got around to me, my eyes dropped to the turquoise tablecloth. "It was f-f-fine," I swallowed, not willing to tell my day's far-from-fine adventure.

That day after school, following the instructions of Sister Ann Teresa, I had walked down the hall to my old first-grade classroom at the Holy Rosary School, the classroom ruled by mean Sister Stella Marie. Not sure why I should be going back to the first-grade classroom, I hesitantly pushed against the red metal door. It opened into a scene from a childhood horror film. The only other children in the room were Ellen Mulvaney (not her real name), known as "the retarded girl," and Rudy Valentino (really his name, but no relation to the Rudolph Valentino of silent screen fame. Rudy lived in West New York, New Jersey, and spoke not a word of English). I looked at Ellen, then at Rudy, and my happy world screeched to a halt louder than fingernails on a blackboard. *Oh no*, I thought, *I've been found out!*

Sister Stella Marie pointed with her ruler to the desk between Ellen and Rudy. It was the same green ruler she had used to whack my neck in first grade when I couldn't figure out the answer to an arithmetic problem at the blackboard. I put my books on the metal rack under the seat and sat down. She pulled at her starched white collar, buried her hands into her draping black sleeves, and glowered: "You children can't read. And I'm going to teach you how."

While Sister read from the first-grade *Dick and Jane* reader, my mind immediately wandered down the hall and out of the building. Mr. Colontoni, our milkman (we called him "Fat Ray Joe Potty Macaroni Colontoni"), had given me an empty milk bottle that morning, and I had the bottle and a ball of yarn in the basket of my blue bike. I was going to the Hudson River to catch a big fish. (Well, okay, a silver guppy. But magnified in the bottle, it would *look* like a big fish.) I was going to put it in a glass bowl, hide it under Ellen's bed, and keep it as a pet.

"Well, Barbara Ann?" Sister Stella Marie interrupted my daydream. "Can you read the next page, please?"

Not wanting to admit I didn't know what page she was on, I told her, "No." Sister leaned over, close enough for me to see the black hairs twitching on her chin. "Barbara Ann, if you don't pay attention," she scowled, *"you'll always be stupid."*

I sucked in my breath, counted to a hundred, and concentrated hard so the tears burning my eyes wouldn't leak out. After class, I cried my way back to our house on Undercliff Avenue, ran up to the woods, and sat on my big rock by the stream. I just knew I would *never* learn to read. Every time I guessed, I was wrong. And when I knew I was right, I was wrong. It wasn't that I wanted to daydream; it just always happened. I couldn't understand the words unless they were read to me: *b* always looked like *d*, *p* looked like *g*, and *e* just looked weird. When I tried to read, my brain was like our Christmas-tree lights that went out when one of the bulbs went bad.

I stifled my tears in time for dinner, not wanting anyone to know that Sister Stella Marie thought I was stupid. How could I be? I was the family entertainer, I created the games, and I was the director of all our basement Broadway shows! I *had* to be brilliant! I *couldn't* be stupid. *Could I?*

After the table was cleared, my mom asked me to stay with her in the kitchen. "I got a call today from Sister Stella Marie, Barbara Ann," she told me while sweeping the floor. "She said you're having trouble reading." I said nothing, but my eyes welled with tears. Mom put down the broom, held my shoulders with both hands, and looked lovingly into my eyes. "Barbara Ann," she said encouragingly, "don't you worry about it. You have a *wonderful imagination*. And with it, you can fill in *any* blanks."

She smiled and picked up her broom.

I knew I had to use my imagination to fill in the blanks with my customer the next day. Combing through the *Times* that evening in the new apartment I shared with Ray, I realized that the New York market was changing. I had been so busy hustling rentals over the last two years, I hadn't noticed that the "For Sale" section of the paper had grown larger than the "Rental" section. Over half the classifieds formerly "For Rent" were now being offered "For Sale."

The whole town seemed to be going co-op. The city's long-standing rent control laws had slowly strangled landlords' profits, pushing them to find a new way to make money. The answer was an "only in New York" harebrained scheme of selling apartments on a cooperative basis. This meant that the buyers of co-ops didn't own their apartments outright, as with condominiums. Instead, they owned shares in the building. Condos were the norm everywhere else in the world; New York just had to be different.

I picked up my phone and called the first two-bedroom apartment that was advertised by its owner—a RIV VU, 2 BR on Sutton Place—and began what would become my standard sales pitch:

"Hello, this is Barbara Corcoran of Corcoran-Simone Real Estate. I'm working with a wonderful young engineer from Union Carbide who has been transferred to New York. He's in town for only one day and needs to buy an apartment tomorrow at the latest. He's asked me for an apartment with . . ." Then I read the seller the detailed description from his own ad, and he responded that his apartment sounded "just like that!"

"I know this might be a terrible imposition," I talked on, "but could I possibly show my customer your apartment at either nine-fifteen or nine-thirty tomorrow morning?"

After the seller agreed to the appointment, I bubbled him with thank-you's and ended the conversation with what would soon become my "Oh-and-by-the-way-just-one-more-question" Columbo close: a few last-second queries guaranteed to ferret out just how negotiable the price really was.

"Oh and by the way," I quickly asked the now excited seller, "have you had many offers on your apartment? Well, has it been on the market very long? Oh, really? Where will you be moving to? Oh, congratulations! When are you expecting to close? Wonderful! I really look forward to seeing you tomorrow at nine-fifteen." If the apartment turned out to be what my customer was actually looking for, I knew I was armed to close.

By the time I finished combing the paper that night and working my sales pitch, I had twelve appointments set. Four were with non-negotiable sellers, six with folks who would take something less than their price, and two with gotta-get-outta-here-fast sellers.

* * *

God was my cobroker when my customer and I walked into the lobby of a twenty-story prewar on East Eighty-fourth Street. Apartment 9K was our eighth apartment of the day, and as we walked past the doorman, my customer beamed, "My boss just bought in this building!" When I found out his boss was living three floors *below* Apartment 9K, all the rest, as they say, was a piece of cake. The living room was the same cocoa brown as my customer's living room in St. Louis, and the seller's boxes were packed by the door ready to go.

By the time I dropped my customer at the Drake it was four o'clock. His flight was at seven. I circled back to the Hayman and Sumner stationery store, picked up a standard Blumberg sales contract, and rushed back to the tiny office Ray and I had taken in a building on East Sixtieth Street. I pecked out the needed information on my new IBM Selectric and circled back to the Drake. My customer was waiting. We jumped in a cab and headed to LaGuardia Airport.

The cab had reached the airport exit when my customer looked up from the contract and asked the question that bedevils every real estate broker in New York:

"Just what *is* a co-op anyway?"

"It's what makes New York so special," I began, never having explained these details and having no idea how I would. "You'll be a sharecropper—I mean shareholder. That means the apartment is yours, but you don't really own it." His eyebrow cocked slightly. "Well, you own it, but you don't get a 'deed.' Instead, you get a 'lease.' But the great thing about a co-op lease is that there's absolutely no rent, just a monthly maintenance fee, which covers all the salaries of the super and the doormen. And the great thing about that is with a few hundred dollars at Christmas, they'll fix anything.

"And then there's the co-op's board of directors," I talked on, "a group of your neighbors whose job is to protect you." His eyebrow relaxed. "They decide what you can and can't do, can and can't change, and who you can and can't sell to because that's what they're not paid to do. If you want to put in a dishwasher, they'll make sure it'll work by having the building's engineer review the plans your architect submits. He'll bill you by the hour and tell you that you can't do it." His eyebrow climbed back up his forehead. "But don't worry. As your boss probably knows already, you can pay the super to sneak it in, just make sure it's in a box that doesn't say 'dishwasher.'"

I could tell by the look on his face I needed to backpedal. "In short, a co-op is a one-of-a-kind thing and when you decide to sell the apartment, you have the right to sell it to whomever you want as long as all your neighbors like the person you want to sell it to. Your buyer, just like you do, will have to submit a list of all his personal assets, liabilities, and income. And six full copies of his last two years' tax returns. You have all those things, right?"

His eyes glazed over. I passed him a pen.

"Sign here."

*

MOM'S LESSON #4: Use your imagination to fill in the blanks.

*

THE LESSON LEARNED ABOUT UNDERLINING THE POSITIVE

When I started my business, I saw myself as the "Queen of New York Real Estate." I pictured myself in great detail, including the clothes I'd wear to address an audience of thousands of people eager to hear my expert advice. I imagined a long line of people waiting to kiss my ring, just as I had seen them kissing the pope's ring on TV. Although I never had an official business plan, my imagination provided a crystal-clear picture of where I wanted to go.

As a kid, I was made to feel like an outsider because I was different. In business, I've become known as an innovator **because** of that difference. What Sister Stella Marie called "stupid," I would later discover was "dyslexic." I've since learned that children who struggle with written information and facts almost always have great imaginations. They can see the big picture, think outside the box, and with just a little encouragement, can learn to use their fertile imaginations to fill in the blanks. Although I'm still a painfully slow reader, I can read a person, size up a situation, and invent a new idea quicker than a wink.

My mother was wise enough to identify my special gift of creativity and underline it. In doing so, she turned my "stupidity" into my greatest strength. I've succeeded because of my learning difference, not despite it.

5

Offer the Bigger Piece, and Yours Will Taste Even Better

1976. Hackensack, New Jersey.

As it turns out, my boyfriend was never really Ramòne Simòne from the Basque Country. He was really Ray Simon from West 185th Street.

I found this out when his development business went bust and we moved from the Manhattan apartment that we shared into his mom's house on Main Street in Hackensack. The house was vintage New Jersey, a two-story asbestos-sided "colonial" with a purple bathtub in the kitchen. In the morning, Ray's mother, Vicki, strained our coffee through a white athletic sock and at night she made us chicken and rice with black beans and plantains. After dinner, I helped her with her job of restringing pearls.

Night after night, we cleared the dishes and Vicki covered the kitchen table with a dark terry-cloth towel. She dumped a sandwich bag full of pearls for each of us, and then we began our three hours of work together. With a pair of small pointed scissors, I clipped the pearls from their original strand, washed them in a small bowl filled with soapy water, and rolled them dry on the towel. Next, I laid out the pearls in size order, the biggest in the middle, the smallest at the ends, and threaded each pearl on a white silk string using a thin wire needle. I tied a knot tightly and evenly against each pearl, locking it into place, until I completed a perfect strand.

One night while stringing, Vicki told me that Ray had taken the name of her third husband, Mr. Simon.

"Simon?" I asked, an errant pearl hitting her linoleum with a *tink*. "I thought it was 'Simòne.' "

"Oh no, his name was 'Simon.' He was from 185th Street and Amsterdam Avenue."

A few months later, Ray's mom gave her son a second chance as a developer by letting him put a second mortgage on her vintage colonial on Main Street.

When Ray got back on his feet, his two oldest daughters came to live with us. We moved out of Vicki's house in Hackensack and into a new high-rise apartment in Fort Lee, not far from the Fort Lee Diner. Each morning, I drove across the George Washington Bridge into Manhattan and each night I returned home in time to make dinner.

In my awkward new role as stepmom, I regularly sat at the dining room table helping Ray's daughters with their homework. His eleven-year-old, Laura, was having trouble reading, so I recounted the story of Sister Stella Marie and tried to do what my mom had done for me. "Laura, don't worry about it," I told her. "You're a very hard worker, and that will get you through almost anything. Besides, you're so good with the big words, I bet one day you'll be a doctor!" Seeing her face light up made the many nights of doing homework worthwhile.

Ray rarely came into the Corcoran-Simone office anymore, other than to sign checks. He was working late more frequently, often meeting with his carpenters, plumbers, and electricians. But he always got home in time to kiss the girls good-night. One Tuesday, Ray came home unusually early, at 6:30. I was in the kitchen pulling the spaghetti off the stove.

"I have something I need to speak with you about," he told me seriously.

"Sure," I said, dumping the spaghetti into the colander.

"I'm going to marry Tina." My hands went limp, and I sloshed the spaghetti into the sink.

"*Tina?* Tina, my *secretary?*" I stammered. "I-I don't understand."

He shifted his weight and put his hands in his pockets. "I guess you should start looking for an apartment or something," he continued. "But take your time."

"It'll take five minutes" was all I could muster.

The next morning, I couldn't lift my head, and my feet couldn't make it onto the small rug beside my friend Catherine's sofa. I was too proud to call my mom and tell her she'd been right all along. For the first time in my life, I called in sick.

I questioned my value without Ray. I traced over the details of our last year together, searching for the signs that should have given me an idea of what was going on. I was filled with anger. I hated Tina. I hated Ray. But, most of all, I hated me.

A few days later, Catherine came over to the sofa with her home remedy for puffy eyes. "Now, Barbara," she began, as I lay mummified on her quilted sofa, "today is the day you're going back to work!" She put two soggy tea bags on my eyes and made a feeble attempt at a pep talk, intermittently spooning more warm water on the tea bags. An hour later, I stumbled to the shower, and for the first time in days, looked in the mirror. I looked just like a raccoon.

"Catherine?" I yelped. "What kind of tea was that?"

There was a long silence in the living room. "Oh my God!" she finally yelled back. "It's Bigelow Blackberry!"

Six coats of Maybelline Coverstick and a whole lot of coaxing later, I put on a don't-notice-me beige outfit—beige blouse, beige pants, and beige shoes—and walked to my office on East Fifty-eighth Street.

I hesitantly stepped off the elevator, sucked in a long, slow breath, and marched into the sea of fourteen sales desks and salespeople facing me at the door. Everyone looked up. I had no idea what they knew, so I smiled my best smile and made a beeline for my office. "Good morning, Norma! Hello, Esther!" I waved as my eyes worked hard to avoid Tina's desk. Then I lost connection with my legs, and I tripped—no, flopped—onto the floor, a sprawled blur of embarrassed beige.

Of course, Tina got to me first. "Are you okay, Barbara?" Ray's fiancée asked kindly. "You look like you hurt your knee."

I knew my mother's red blotches were forming on my chest, and I was grateful for the beige turtleneck. "I'm fine," I stammered, groping for the contents of my purse. "I'm fine!" I grabbed for my subway tokens and tampons as they rolled to the far reaches. "My purse is fine, my knee is fine, *everything's just fine!*"

A phone rang, providing the needed distraction for me to limp into the office I shared with Ray.

"Tina can't work for Corcoran-Simone anymore," I announced to Ray.

"Tina's staying," Ray informed me. "Remember, Barbara, I'm the majority partner here, owning fifty-one percent, and that puts me in control of this business."

Our romance had died a sudden death, but it would be a long time before we broke up the business. Somehow, I plowed through the next year and a half of entrances and smiles just fine, while slowly building the courage to walk away from Ray for good. One Thursday afternoon, as we made our usual weekly deposit at the bank, it hit me—now was the time.

"Ray," I said, "I'm going to start my own company."

His left eye twitched beneath his blue aviator shades, but he remained calm. "You might want to give that a little more thought," he suggested.

So I did. Overnight. And what I thought was this: *I actually know what I'm doing and I can do it without him.* But how to leave him gracefully had me stumped.

Lying in bed that night, I decided to suggest we divide our business the way my mom did her cake.

Sunday night. Edgewater.

Mom made our favorite dessert on Sunday nights, a Duncan Hines Devil's Food Cake in a rectangular aluminum pan. After dinner, Mom placed the warm cake on top of two waffle-weave dish towels in the middle of the table, and we watched and drooled as she cut it into twelve pieces using the flat edge of her spatula. As we went around the table, each child eyed and vied for the biggest piece.

When there were only two pieces left, it was Eddie's turn to pick, and he reached for the bigger of the two. "Eddie!" Mom interrupted. "Let your sister Ellen go first."

Mom had a rule that when there were two pieces left of anything, we had to offer the bigger piece to the other person. She insisted it made our piece taste better.

Ellen, who was toiling away at the dishes in the sink like the Good Housekeeping Seal come to life, wiped her hands, marched over to the table, and picked exactly the piece Eddie wanted.

"Don't worry, Eddie," Mom reminded him, "now *yours* will taste even better!"

I've got to offer Ray the "bigger piece," I concluded. I turned off the light and went to sleep.

Ray was spending a lot more time at the office, and when he arrived the next afternoon, I was ready for him.

"There's something serious I need to talk to you about," I said as he settled into his black leather chair. "I've given things a lot of thought, Ray, and I *am* going to open my own business." I waited, but he said nothing. "So, we have to decide how to divide up the company. We'll need to establish two separate bank accounts and split the receivables and the cash. One of us can keep the office, but one of us will have to move. We'll each need our own phone number." Ray sat silent. "And since we have fourteen salespeople, we can each take seven. I suggest we do a football-type draw, and since you're the majority shareholder, you should get to pick first." Ray seemed pleased with the "you pick first" terms.

I had already reviewed the list of salespeople and knew I needed Esther to help me move my business forward. For me, Esther was indispensable. I figured if I went first and picked her, Ray might argue for her.

"Okay," he began. "I'll take Norma." Norma was clearly the big moneymaker. She was our top-producing salesperson, and her sales alone accounted for 60 percent of our company's commissions. And, now, Norma and her 60 percent were Ray's.

"Okay, then," I said, "I'll take Esther." Esther wasn't our top moneymaker, but she was a consistent producer and had all the traits I needed to build my new business. Esther was smart, organized, and worked twice as hard as everyone else.

We went back and forth until we had divided up the remaining dozen people.

"I'll keep the main '355-1200' phone number," Ray declared. Ray always said our number was a "very important number" and made the company sound big.

"Then I'll take the new number," I agreed. I knew Ray would think 355-3550 sounded less important, but it was snappy, and I thought far easier to remember.

"And I'll stay here," Ray concluded, "and *you'll* have to move." I nodded. Although it would be expensive to move, I knew it would be a fresh start. The same space was available upstairs with a lot more light, and I could rent it for the same amount of money.

We had finished all our business, so I put my calendar into my shoulder bag and zipped it up. "What will you call your company, Ray?" I asked, standing near the door.

"Pogue-Simone, of course!" he bragged. *How romantic*, I thought painfully, but quickly comforted myself when I realized that people would have a hard time spelling or pronouncing Tina's last name anyway.

"Well, Ray," I announced, "I'm going to call *my* new company '*The Corcoran Group.*'" And as I said it, I knew it was right.

We shook hands. Ray was obviously pleased with the results and was relishing what he viewed as a clear win through and through. He got up, walked past me, and turned around. "You know, Barb," he said, putting his hands in his pockets, "*you'll never succeed without me.*" And with that, Ramòne Simòne strutted away.

I leaned back on my old desk, the one Ray had just picked for Tina, and vowed to myself that I would rather *die* than let him see me fail!

✳

MOM'S LESSON #5: Offer the bigger piece, and yours will taste even better.

✳

THE LESSON LEARNED ABOUT PIE-SPLITTING

It took almost eighteen months for me to build the courage to leave Ramòne Simòne, as I still believed my success depended on him. Once I offered Ray the bigger piece, it was easier to leave, because I knew I had been more than fair.

As the majority shareholder, Ray was entitled to 51 percent of the money. That was obvious. But I knew that Ray, if given the choice, would reach for the immediate gratification of getting the top-producing salesperson. I got the longer-term better pick by choosing Esther.

I've found that whenever I offered the other guy the bigger piece, I got what I wanted and it always tasted better.

6

Put the Socks in the
Sock Drawer

1978. The Corcoran Group. Three days before opening.

"*No!*" I shrieked as I opened the door into a forest of six-foot cartons. I squeezed through the cardboard hulks, waded through a sea of spilled manila, and picked up a handful of scattered Bic pens. Gawking at the pyramid of tangled chair legs that the Nice Jewish Boy Movers had piled in the middle of my spanking-new office, I worried aloud, *"How the heck am I going to pull this off?"*

I had rented an office three flights above the offices of Pogue-Simone, leaving the Kelly-green walls, dented black desks, and makeup-smeared phones for Tina and Ray. Instead of buying furniture and equipment, I had decided to lease new phones, typewriters, and desks, to stretch my $14,837.14 half of the Corcoran-Simone money as far as it would go. I splurged the extra eleven bucks a month for charcoal-gray desks instead of the standard-issue black ones, and paid a little extra to paint the walls a fancy cranberry instead of institutional white.

Trying to swallow my anxiety along with my breakfast, I looked back at the door and thought, *I just don't have enough time, money, or help, and in three days I'm going to have a whole lot of salespeople with a whole lot of needs, walking right through that door!*

For the first time in my life, I felt really alone. I put my coffee aside and thought about calling my mom, but I didn't. Ever since I left home with Ray against her wishes, I had been determined not to need her anymore.

I glanced at my watch. It was 6:30 A.M. Mom would be beginning her morning routine about now. I could see her running through the house putting everything in order, and I wished she could be here with me to whip everything into shape. She'd know exactly what to do.

School day. Edgewater.

"Good morning, everyone!" Mom's voice boomed as she ripped the covers from each of our beds. Dazed, I made my way to the kitchen table, took a cereal bowl from the stack, and stumbled to the stove for my one scoop of hot Quaker Oats.

"Good morning, Mom," I mumbled.

"Good morning, Barbara Ann," she smiled back.

I sat down as I always did in my assigned seat next to the bathroom door, and stirred milk and brown sugar into my oatmeal as it cooled. My brothers and sisters were all doing the same. At 7:00 A.M. sharp, with only three spoonfuls to go, Mom declared breakfast over. We had twenty minutes to wait in line for the bathroom to brush our teeth and comb our hair, and then put on the clothes Mom had placed at the foot of our beds.

"Where's my socks?" Eddie yelled to no one.

"Where's my socks?" was a question you only asked once in our house. Every sock in our house was stored in the two square drawers on the skinny wall between the bathroom and the stove. The top

drawer was filled with the girls' white nylon socks, and the bottom
with the boys' navy cotton socks.

Mom pulled Eddie by his ear into the kitchen, opened the bottom sock drawer, and pointed.

"Socks," she pronounced slowly with emphasis, "are *always* in
the sock drawer." She left Eddie rubbing his ear and darted off to
sort the laundry.

My mother had a routine for everything. When she sorted the
laundry, she started by dumping it all in the middle of the living
room floor. Then she divided it into the "white pile" and the "color
pile," and subdivided those into "heavy" and "light" fabrics. Next,
she placed the four piles atop four dirty bedsheets, tied a knot in
each, and slung them two-to-a-shoulder into the kitchen. By day's
end, Mom sorted, washed, hung, folded, and put away eight loads of
laundry.

She prepared for school mornings the night before, painting our
white bucks on top of the living room radiator with Kiwi shoe polish
and her two-inch Sherwin-Williams paintbrush. Early on, she
painted the radiator white so her late-night drips wouldn't show.

Then Mom made our lunches in less than two minutes. First, she
plopped a tub of Skippy peanut butter, a jar of Welch's grape jelly,
and a five-pound bag of McIntosh apples on the kitchen table. She
dealt out twenty slices of Wonder Bread into two perfectly parallel
rows and, with her ten-inch icing knife, spread the top row with
peanut butter and the bottom row with jelly. Then she flipped the
top slices onto the bottoms, halved each sandwich on the diagonal,
and wrapped each in waxed paper. After punching open ten brown
paper bags, Mom dropped a sandwich and an apple inside. At noon
the next day, we opened our bags to find one apple and a concave
peanut butter and jelly on white.

"C'mon, c'mon!" Mom yelled to us every morning at 7:20, as
she stood by the door guarding our white bucks warming in size
order beneath the radiator. "Hurry or you're going to be late!"

We slid in our socked feet across the turquoise tile of the living room, dropped into our white bucks, grabbed a lunch bag, and headed out the door.

After I thought about the systems that made my mother's house work, I knew the only chance I had of having a well-run office rested on having a place and a system for everything. So, I spent the weekend planning and getting organized.

First, I made a list of everything that *didn't* work at the old office, a long list of time-wasters, and figured out how to eliminate them. Then, I made a list of what *did* work and devised ways to do them even better. I thought through my salespeople's office needs, numbered the most important ones, and crossed out the ones that could wait. I tore the lists from my yellow legal pad and hailed a cab over to Hayman and Sumner stationers. I browsed through the merchandise, sizing up its usefulness, and came home with a large carton full of file folders, colored index cards, and labels.

9:15 A.M. The Corcoran Group. First day.

"Good morning," I said as each of my seven salespeople cautiously walked through the door. "After you hang up your coat, please come over here, reach in, and pull out a number." I had numbered and folded fourteen pieces of paper and put them in a red Bloomingdale's shopping bag. Each number in the bag corresponded with a number I had taped to the desks.

Cathy picked first, tentatively reaching into the bag. "Oh, Cathy!" I exclaimed. "Congratulations! You got number seven! You picked the *best* desk here!" David was next and pulled out number three. "Is that number three you have there, David?" I gushed. "Congratulations, David! *You* picked the best desk here."

The number I was pulling had everyone laughing.

"Now, remember," I shouted into the excited sales area, "if you don't like your desk, don't even give it a moment's thought, because we'll be changing all our seats in six months anyway! And if you do like your desk, don't get used to it, because we'll be changing all our seats in six months anyway! And please don't put your things on the empty desk next to yours, because we'll be filling that seat in no time at all."

On each of the seven assigned desks, I had placed a small yellow rose in a white vase with a handwritten note. The salespeople settled in and smiled as they read, "I'm so happy you're here! xoxo—Barb."

I spotted John Bachman about to post his cardboard DO NOT DIS-TURB sign high above desk number five. From his perfectly parted blond hair to his stiff ironing-board walk, everything about John said, "Leave me alone."

I approached cautiously. "John?" I interrupted. "You may have needed that DO NOT DISTURB sign in our old office, but you won't need it around here. In this office, *everyone* can disturb *everyone*."

John turned his starched neck, twisted his pinky ring a half-turn to the right, and nodded, "Vell, if zat's vat you vant . . ." And took down the sign.

I walked to the front of the office and shouted, "Okay, now, please get yourself a cup of coffee and a doughnut, and we'll start our meeting." While they sugared, milked, and stirred, I began. "Good morning, everyone!"

Everyone humored me and chimed back, "Good morning, Barbara."

"Today, I have six announcements to make, and the first is that we're going to have breakfast here together every Monday morning. It will begin at nine-thirty and end promptly at ten-fifteen." Everyone looked around at each other and seemed pleased.

"The second announcement is that we'll be starting a new system for our listing information, and here's how the system will work." I held up four different-colored index cards. "The new listing cards carry the same property information as our old ones did, but the new colors will make it easier to find the right-size apartment when you need it." I demonstrated each color as I spoke. "All studio apartment information will be written on the white cards, all one-bedrooms on the yellow cards, two-bedrooms on blue, and three-bedrooms and larger will always be pink. Every time you get a new listing, you'll write it on the appropriate colored card and file it in the corresponding colored box. As our new listing system helps everyone, no one will receive listing credit if the apartment is written on the wrong-colored card."

I smiled and nodded, and everyone nodded along.

"The third announcement is about getting better property information. I'm sure you all agree that the more we know about each property, the better chance we have of selling it. So, from now on, I'll be paying cash for better information. For example, when David writes up all the details about his new listing, and Sandy, after seeing it, is able to add one more fact to David's information, I'll give Sandy one dollar for helping David." I waved a fistful of dollars in the air and smiled.

Everyone smiled back.

"Announcement four is about the form you fill out to get your commissions." I held up the familiar eight-by-eleven sheet of paper. "Well, now, the commission request form is green and it has a back side." I flipped it over, showing the list of questions I had worked hours to create. "When you answer the questions on the back, we'll all have a much better idea of where our business is actually coming from.

"For example, where did you get the customer? Did they call you on a Sunday ad? Find you in an open house? Or were they referred by a friend or business associate? Simply check a box. Where is your customer living now? Is he here in the city? Or is he moving from another state? Another country? Or another planet? Check a box. And what business is your customer in? Is he married? Single? Children? How old is he? Simply check a box. Knowing where our business is coming from will help us get more business."

Everyone nodded along with me.

"If we know more about our sellers and how each deal was made," I continued, "we'll all be much better negotiators. So some of the other questions are about the sale itself. How long was the property on the market before it sold? What was the first offer? And how much was negotiated before the deal was done?

"The new commission form will take only three minutes to complete. All you have to do is check the appropriate boxes. Commissions will be paid every Friday, and no commission will be paid without it."

Everyone nodded. So I went on: "Do you remember back at Corcoran-Simone when we desperately looked for floor plans while our customers waited in the lobby? Do you remember the day we actually dumped out John's drawer looking for the floor plan of his new listing at 2 Sutton Place? After today, here at The Corcoran Group, we're never going to search for a lost floor plan again. Because now, when you get a floor plan for your new listing, you'll immediately create a 'floor plan folder' for *everyone* to use."

I stood and waved a sample folder for everyone to see, and demonstrated.

"First, before the floor plan can get lost, you staple the new floor plan to the inside of a manila folder and print the address boldly on the folder's tab." I walked over to the copy machine, placed the file facedown, and pressed the print button. "Next, you make ten copies of the original and put them inside the folder. Then you place the floor plan file by street order in the new 'floor plan drawer' at the front of the office. Remember, if you take the last copy from the folder, you're the one responsible for using the stapled original to make ten more copies." As the copy machine finished, I said, "Ta-dah!! No more lost floor plans."

Everyone nodded.

"And this brings us to our last announcement, the 'Good Idea Box.'" I pulled out a cardboard shoebox on which I had drawn a giant yellow lightbulb. "This box is for *Good Ideas*," I enunciated. "Whenever you have an idea, I'd like to know about it. I don't care if it's a big idea, small idea, or even a stupid idea—all ideas are welcome! I'll pay five dollars for every idea, and I'll even give you five bucks for a complaint—but only if it's accompanied by a solution. So, here's the first five bucks for John Bachman, who suggested only ten minutes ago that we eliminate the DO NOT DISTURB signs from the office. Great job, John!" I said, and placed the money in his limp hand.

I looked around the room, took a breath, and asked, "Does anyone have any questions?" Seven dazed salespeople shook their heads no. "Okay, then, I guess that's everything. The Monday meeting is now over."

The phone rang, I reached over the reception desk, and answered, "Good morning, The Corcoran Group."

※

MOM'S LESSON #6: Put the socks in the sock drawer.

※

THE LESSON LEARNED ABOUT ORGANIZING A BUSINESS

Good systems make plans happen. Here's how the organizational systems introduced at the first Corcoran Group sales meeting would help build my business over the next twenty-five years.

1. Check the Box

The commission request form enabled me to get an unprecedented amount of information from my sales agents. Like other independent contractors, real estate agents closely guard information related to their clients. But they willingly gave me the information simply because I made the process easy and because they wouldn't get paid without it.

In New York, change happens in a New York minute, and the back side of my commission request form captured it as it happened.

Here are three ways to use the power of information to help build a business:

Early information helps predict emerging markets.

New York's a town where there's always someone coming and someone going, and the answers my salespeople consistently provided on the commission request form enabled me to stay ahead of those changes.

In the late seventies, my little checked boxes helped predict the emergence of Manhattan's "new" West Side. For decades, property values on the West Side had trailed far behind those of the East Side, but in 1979, the margin narrowed dramatically, almost overnight. The answers my sales agents provided showed that the customers moving to the West Side were the children of affluent parents on the East Side, and the young "thirtysomethings" were fast becoming the norm. Although everybody said I was crazy, I immediately opened a huge West Side office and was positioned to ride the crest of the wave.

Information positions your company as the reliable source for facts and figures.

Our Corcoran Group offices became a veritable research center for the numbers-hungry New York press because when a reporter called, I had the answer. And the press called us for information on everything, including stories that had nothing to do with real estate. If a reporter wanted to talk to a young Czechoslovakian metal sculptor living in a Greenwich Village walk-up, we could find him in twenty minutes or less. And today, with the advent of e-mail, we can do it in ten.

Tracking the source of your customers helps you spend your advertising dollars wisely.
Most real estate advertising money is spent in the Sunday classified section of the local newspaper. By knowing which ads produced the most customers we were able to redirect our advertising dollars as the business changed, placing different-size ads in different publications on different days of the week.

In short, the back side of the commission request form told me everything I needed to know to reach my target market, place effective advertising, and grab media attention while doing it.

2. Meet on Monday

People don't read memos, but they'll listen to a big mouth.

Every Corcoran Group office has a Monday-morning meeting that serves multiple functions. It gets salespeople out of bed and into the office, and is the single best vehicle for communicating information, broadcasting sales, and promoting new properties. It's also the best arena to publicly recognize individual success within a peer group.

The Monday meeting is the business equivalent of my mother's kitchen table.

3. Please *Do* Disturb

In a real estate office, the agent at the next desk is as much a competitor as a colleague. John Bachman used his DO NOT DISTURB sign to keep people out of his business and away from his desk, preventing any exchange of information and ideas. My early redirection of John with my "everyone *can* disturb everyone" philosophy became a cornerstone of our company's commitment to teamwork. It was also the beginning of our company's open-door policy. Today at our Corcoran Group offices there are no locked doors or drawers, and the only walls are made of glass.

4. Pick a Number

Fair is fair. From the first day of business, I made sure not to pick favorites. Everyone needs to know what the rules are and that everyone is playing by them. In our first office, everyone was given the same opportunity to pick the "best" desk, and in subsequent offices, sales desks were picked in order of sales production, the biggest producer picking first.

Fair play is the best way in every situation. In the spring of 1998, I chaired and was host to twelve hundred corporate presidents from around the world for a business conference at the elegant Plaza Hotel. My guests were to stay at the hotel for a week and had booked their rooms at the same, although very expensive, room rate. Some of the suites had better views, some were on better floors, and some were better appointed. Instead of allowing the hotel staff to assign the rooms to the guests as they normally did, I insisted the attendees randomly pick a plastic ball out of three-foot silver goblets. Each ball was marked with a room number.

Not everyone stayed in the penthouse, but everyone slept well. And as the host, I averted a week of complaints because the presidents had all picked their own rooms within the context of fair play.

5. Color Code

People misread labels and misfile the alphabet, but very few people are color-blind. The new colored listing cards and floor plan files made missing information easier to find and more difficult to hide. By 1980, the colored listing cards would become New York City's first real estate database, and by 1994 would convert again into our corcoran.com Web site, which today is the city's

leading real estate Web site, selling more than $700 million in
real estate annually.

6. Write Notes/Give Flowers

Little things pave the road to loyalty.

No one is too sophisticated to appreciate a small individual
expression of affection. To employees, it's money in the bank
with interest. To employers, the gift is truly in the giving.

7. Make a "Good Idea" Box

My little shoebox with the yellow lightbulb drawn on top became
my best source of bright ideas. Although many ideas were down-
right impossible, the ideas poured in and among them I found
nuggets of gold.

In business, the clerical people are rarely solicited for their
opinions and ideas. But our Good Idea Box was an equal-
opportunity listener, giving everyone the assurance they would
be heard. It allowed every individual to be a contributor, feel a
part of the team, and make five bucks.

The best creative ideas often came from the clerical staff, and
the best operational ideas usually came from the salespeople.
The box also gave me an early "heads up" on what was about to
go awry, well before it matured into a big problem.

I didn't just preach the Good Idea Box, I used it. And it
guaranteed success.

The simple systems I introduced at our first Monday meeting gave
The Corcoran Group the footing it needed to start building a solid
company. And those good ideas can all be attributed to the simple
genius of my mother's good planning.

7

If There's More Than One Kid to Wash, Set Up a Bathtime Routine

Second week. The Corcoran Group.

"'Seven salespeople needed . . .'" I read the words of my help wanted ad to the phone operator at the *New York Times* and realized I sounded desperate. "Wow," I said, "when you read it out loud, 'needed' sounds really *needy*, doesn't it?" The operator said nothing. "Let me change it to 'Seven desks are awaiting.'" I heard her fingers typing. "Is 'awaiting' a word?" I asked. She said nothing. I looked down at the many versions of the ad I had scratched out on my pad and figured I'd better rethink my approach. "You know what? I'll call you back."

In fact, I saw I had two problems to solve. First, I had to attract enough applicants to give me a good chance to choose good hires. Second, I knew I couldn't let potential salespeople see us as we were, *desperate* to fill seven desks! I needed a way to make the good candidates *want* us.

Saturday night. The front steps.

"Who wants to go to the Dairy Queen?" Dad asked us as we gathered on the front steps.

"Me! Me!" we raised our hands and chimed in unison.

"Who wants to get a cold, chocolate Dilly Bar?" Dad continued. "Or maybe an extra-thick frozen strawberry milk shake in a big white cup with a straw to suck it all up?"

"Me! Me! I would, Dad!" every voice begged.

"Or maybe," he tempted further, "a double banana float with big scoops of chocolate, butter pecan, and strawberry ice cream, all covered with caramel syrup and a big pile of whipped cream?"

"Me! Dad, me! I would!" we all chimed in. Denise jumped up. John pushed Tommy aside so his hand could be better seen, and Ellen clambered onto Dad's lap.

Dad had our attention, and we waited with drooling mouths for his next words.

"Well, kids," Dad smiled, putting his arms around Ellen and me, "so would I. Yep, that sure would be nice, but . . . not tonight, kids. Maybe *next* week."

Denise sat down, John dropped his hand, and Ellen slumped against Dad's chest.

The next Saturday, though, Dad smiled and said, "So would I! *Get in the car, kids!*" And the chocolate Dilly Bar was even sweeter, because we'd been made to want it even more.

I thought about Dad's Dairy Queen tease and dialed the *New York Times*.

"Hello, are you the same operator I was just speaking to?" I asked the voice on the other end of the line. "Oh, well, anyway, I'd like to place a help wanted ad in this Sunday's paper." And I read:

I knew the ad would work.

I opened my calendar and cleared my Monday-morning schedule. Now to deal with the next problem. When the phone started ringing, I was going to need one heck of a routine to take the calls, interview the salespeople, and hire the right ones.

Bath time. The Corcoran kitchen.

"Thank you, God," Mom prayed each night as she soaked in the hot water of what she called the "Holiest tub in Edgewater." "Thank you for giving me the next three minutes for myself." Exactly two minutes and fifty-eight seconds later, Mom jumped out of the tub, threw on her pink robe, and took two broad strides out of the bathroom and into the kitchen. She was ready for the bathtime routine.

She punched the TALK button on the black intercom that Uncle Alan had borrowed from his job at Bell Telephone. "Kids!" her voice squawked, as it did every night on our bedroom speaker. "You have exactly five minutes to finish your homework and report to the kitchen! I repeat, *five* minutes. And, Eddie, leave Johnny alone!"

We all collected in the kitchen and took our place in line next to the refrigerator. Eight-year-old Denise, the oldest, then me, then Eddie, then Ellen, then Johnny holding little Tommy's hand.

Dad was in charge of washing and Mom in charge of rinsing. First up was Denise, who climbed onto the counter next to the double white porcelain sink. Dad slid her into the deep side of the sink filled to the brim with warm sudsy water. Starting with her head, he kneaded the shampoo through her hair, down her back, over her behind, past her legs, and finally between her toes.

When Denise stepped over into the clear water of Mom's rinsing sink, Dad slid me from the counter into the washing sink and began kneading the shampoo into my hair. Mom used her black-handled aluminum pot to give Denise a warm final rinse, and then, like a baton in a relay, quickly passed Denise back off to Dad.

I stepped over into Mom's rinsing sink, and on cue my brother Eddie stepped into the washing sink, where he waited while Dad sat Denise on top of the terry-covered counter and used his big towel to speed-dry her hair. Denise's job was to press her head into Dad's chest as hard as she could, and try to hum *"Aaaaaaah"* straight through the vibration to the very end.

As Denise moved over to the kitchen table to put on the printed flannels Mom had waiting in size order, I was *"aaaaaahing"* through the speed-dry, Eddie was getting Mom's final rinse, Ellen was stepping into Dad's sink, and Johnny and Tommy waited in line.

By the time the calls started coming in on Sunday, I had set up a routine as squeaky-clean as Mom's to move the sales applicants in and out.

"Hello," the first caller pleasantly began, "I'm calling about your empty desk advertisement in today's paper."

Our receptionist responded with "Thank you for calling. If you would just hold a moment, I'll connect you with our president."

As I picked up the phone, the applicant politely repeated, "I'm calling about your empty desk ad in today's paper."

"Oh, thank you for calling," I responded, "but unfortunately that position has already been filled."

"What?" the caller asked suspiciously. "How could that possibly be? It just appeared in today's paper!"

"Yes, and I'm very sorry," I explained sympathetically. "But we usually have a long list of people waiting to join our company, and the positions are often taken before the ad even appears. I'm really sorry to disappoint you."

"Well . . . okay," the caller said, "I guess I understand—"

"But," I interrupted, "positions do open up from time to time, and I'd be happy to get together with you anyway. Then at least we'd have a chance to meet one another so when another position opens, I could call you immediately."

"Oh, would you? That would be very nice of you."

"Tomorrow at ten, then?" I finished.

I narrowed twenty-seven would-be salespeople into sixteen appointments and scheduled them the next morning between 10:00 and 1:00. Each applicant was surprised to find three other people already waiting, and jockeyed for a piece of the small bench at the front of the office.

Our receptionist greeted everyone with a four-page sales application. On my instructions, she gave those who appeared well groomed and well dressed a pen. And those applicants who weren't "dressed for success," she handed a pencil. When the applicants called to follow up later, I had a surefire way to tell which callers to spend my time with.

I scanned each sales application to ferret out the applicant's personal references and home address because the information would tell me whether or not they had the contacts and customer leads I couldn't give them.

The first interview of the day was with a well-coiffed woman in her early forties. After chatting at length about her children, hobbies, and husbands, I corralled the conversation back in with "Mary, I'm so happy you've spent all this time telling me about your family and friends." I smiled and she smiled back. "But would you mind if I'm totally honest with you?"

"Please, of course not," she welcomed.

"Well, Mary, after working with so many different people, I

guess I've concluded that great salespeople have a few things in common. The first is empathy. You know, the ability to get along with people. And, Mary, it's obvious to me that you're very, very good with people. Would you agree?"

Mary straightened her back, sat up proudly, and said, "Yes, of course. Yes, yes, I'm *very* good with people."

I smiled and then paused with obvious concern. "But," I said in a serious voice, "I've also found that the other thing great salespeople share is a real need to succeed—I'd almost call it a killer instinct. And for whatever reason, I'm just not getting it from you." Then I sat back in my chair and waited for her response.

For the next five minutes, Mary gave a monologue on how she "really *was* aggressive." Her words were right, but her music was all wrong.

I bade her good-bye and promised to call if a position became available. It never would.

The next applicant sashayed in with her black alligator briefcase, removed an alligator glove, and extended her manicured hand across my desk. She explained she had "four years' real estate experience" and knew all the right people in all the right places. In three short minutes, she made it perfectly clear to me she had nothing to learn. And I believed her and sent her on her way.

Thirteen applicants later, a tall woman named Emily marched confidently into my office and plopped down. She wore a hot-pink tweed suit trimmed with a contrasting taupe braid. Her suit had more buttons than I had in my whole wardrobe. They were bright gold with two raised *C*'s on each of them. I immediately made a mental note to imitate their design for a Corcoran Group logo.

When I got to my standard "I don't think you're aggressive . . ." line, Emily was so insulted I thought she'd leap across the desk and grab my throat. And as she yap-yap-yapped in my face, I knew Emily was the gal for me.

✳

MOM'S LESSON #7: If's there's more than one kid to wash, set up a bathtime routine.

✳

THE LESSON LEARNED ABOUT SETTING UP GOOD ROUTINES

Although I was desperate to fill seven desks, I created the impression that desks at The Corcoran Group were in short supply. Realizing that good salespeople need to compete, I knew the adrenaline would flow when they were forced to compete for the already taken "One Empty Desk."

When they arrived, the applicants were greeted with a lengthy sales application and a job that was filled. I knew that the higher the hurdle, the more convinced salespeople would be that the other side must be a very important place. My pen-and-pencil routine quickly sorted the professional-looking applicants from the rest, and saved time when they called to follow up.

My "I don't think you're aggressive" challenge became my sure-fire system to pick out the winners. When Emily vehemently reacted to my challenge, I didn't need to listen to her words, because her music came through loud and clear. People can't fake passion.

My hiring routine quickly filled our seven empty desks with exceptional salespeople because, like my mother's bathtime routine, it allowed me to process lots of people in a short time. My new hires gave us the early sales talent that would soon push The Corcoran Group ahead of our competitors.

8

If You Want to Be in Two Places
at Once, Borrow a Reel-to-Reel

Sixth month. The Corcoran Group.

The "empty desk" ad produced more people to start, train, and motivate than I had time to start, train, and motivate.

Each morning, I hit the phones at 8:30 sharp to finish setting up my sales appointments for the day. I was ready by 9:45, when my eager new hurdle-jumpers showed up for their sales training.

We spent the first twenty minutes reviewing our customer cards and dividing them into three piles, based on how urgently each customer needed a place to live. The "hot-to-trot" customers formed the "A" pile, the "I'll-buy-it-when-I-find-it"s were the "B"s, and the "C" rating was reserved for the annoying "I'll-shop-till-I-drop" group. I had each salesperson tear up their "C" customers and toss them in the trash.

For the next forty-five minutes, we called each of our new property listings, asking questions like "When are you moving? Why? When do you need to close?" Then we would rate each seller from least to most motivated and divide them into three piles, labeling them "not negotiable," "will take something less," and "gotta-get-outta-here-fast!"

I worked with my bright-eyed crew until 11:00 A.M., took a minute to tell them how much I appreciated them, and darted out for my showings of the day. Around 6:30, I rushed back to the office to return phone calls and set up my sales appointments for the next morning. Then, as it was the days before cell phones and e-mails, I read through the numerous notes left for me in my "in" box and jotted my responses to the salespeople.

Around 8:00, I locked the door and walked the eleven blocks home to my one-bedroom floor-through on East Sixty-ninth Street. I climbed the stairs to the second floor, turned the double deadbolt lock, took a consoling breath, and opened the door into the only place I had ever lived by myself in my life. I was thankful to be too busy and too exhausted to be lonely.

I knew I couldn't keep up the routine much longer. I knew I needed another me.

Bedtime. The girls' room.

"Eddie!" Mom hollered to Dad. "Eddie, they're ready!"

As the household population grew, Mom ran out of time. In order to give herself the needed minutes each night to prepare for the mornings, Mom was (thankfully) forced to give up her position as one of our two rooms' nightly lullaby singers. She had Dad record his favorite songs on a brown reel-to-reel tape deck that Uncle Alan had borrowed from his job at Bell Telephone. Then she set up Dad to alternate nights between the girls' room and the boys' room, singing songs to lull us to sleep. The room that wasn't getting a live performance could instead listen to *Dad's Greatest Hits.* In so doing, Mom succeeded in putting Dad in two places at once and creating a stand-in for her.

Tonight, Dad was live in the girls' room. He sauntered in with his old wood guitar and sat down on the edge of Ellen's bed. I watched as he carefully removed his pick from between the E, G, and A strings and strummed a single sweet C chord. Denise was the first to blurt out a request: "Sing us the one about 'Heart of my heart,' Dad!"

"And 'Valla-Valla-Vee Was in the Army,'" Ellen quickly added, as she set upright in her bed.

"And what about you, Barbara Ann?" Dad asked. "What will it be tonight?"

I always waited, so I could hear Dad say my name. "My usual," I answered, "'Give My Regards to Hoboken.'"

Dad began to sing in his Perry Como voice. I scrunched the covers up tight against my chin, stretched my toes as far as I could, and fought my heavy eyelids until I heard the very last words of my favorite song.

> *Give my regards to Hoboken,*
> *Down where the breezes blow.*
> *In all kinds of weather,*
> *You'll find us together,*
> *In H-O-B-O-K-E-N, E-N,*
> *In H-O-B-O-K-E-N!*

While Dad crooned in the girls' room and his voice reel-to-reeled in the boys' room, Mom made the next day's lunches in the kitchen.

The day Esther Kaplan arrived for her interview at the old Corcoran-Simone, she wore a two-piece knit dress that was mostly cream and green, with small touches of cranberry. She was a small, elegant woman in her mid-forties and carried a beige handbag with a Bakelite handle and clasp. An executive secretary to a real estate attorney, Esther wanted to make a change in her career.

The first thing Esther did was present her card, which she carefully removed from her purse. I caught a quick glimpse inside.

Esther's handbag was a small miracle of organization, a miniature file cabinet disguised as a fashion accessory. She unzipped one of the two interior pockets, extracted the card, handed it to me, zipped the pocket, and snapped the clasp. Before the interview was over, I knew I'd feel safe with my wallet in Esther's purse.

That's what I remembered as I realized I desperately needed someone to help me run the business. And after working side by side with her for the past two years, I knew I could trust Esther with any amount of responsibility, if she would only agree to take it on. So one night I asked her if she could stay an hour late.

"Esther," I began, "I really appreciate your taking the time out of your busy day to meet with me, and I must say that I'm constantly amazed at what a phenomenal salesperson you are. I remember you made your first sale your very first month at Corcoran-Simone, and I think you've made a sale every month since. I frankly don't know how you do it. Esther, you are truly an amazing lady."

"Thank you, Barb," Esther quietly replied. "That's very nice to hear."

"Esther, I'm wondering if you would consider taking on more of a leadership role here at the company," I continued.

Esther raised a suspicious brow. "What leadership role would that be?"

"Why, the most important position there is, vice president of The Corcoran Group," I heralded.

"And what would the vice president of The Corcoran Group do?" she inquired.

"Basically, you would be an extension of me," I explained. "When I'm out showing apartments, you would act with my full authority. And when you were out showing apartments, I would act in your stead. I guess you could say we'd be one, and together we would build the business."

"Well, Barb, I don't know what to say," she answered, obviously flattered and surprised. "I'll have to give this some serious consideration." She hesitated, clutching her purse closer to her chest. "May I ask what the position would pay?"

I hadn't really thought about this minor point, but suddenly I remembered Wimpy from the Popeye cartoons Mom let us watch on Saturday mornings.

"I would gladly pay you Tuesday for one hamburger today," I said with a smile.

Esther straightened in her chair, tilted her head, and said, "I'm not quite sure I understand."

I laughed. "Esther, I don't have any money to offer you right now, but this is more important than money. I'm offering you a partnership, and I could pay you in stock. In fact, I'll pay you ten percent of our entire stock in three years if you help me build my business today." With that, I took a yellow legal pad from the shelf and drew three wide columns across the top.

The first I labeled "Year." The second, "# of Salespeople." And the last column I labeled "Commissions." I figured my fourteen salespeople would bring in $250,000 this year, so in the first row, I wrote "1978," "14," and "$250,000." Then as Esther watched with interest, I quickly worked down each column, doubling the number of salespeople and commissions on each year as I went.

YEAR	# OF SALESPEOPLE	COMMISSIONS
1978	14	$250,000
1979	28	$500,000
1980	56	$1,000,000
1981	112	$2,000,000
1982	224	$4,000,000
1983	448	$8,000,000
1984	896	$16,000,000
1985	1,792	$32,000,000!!!!!

"Thirty-two million dollars!" I exclaimed when I completed the last row. The number astonished me. I was amazed at how easy it would be to become rich! I looked up at Esther, circled the impressive sum, and gushed, "Well, what do you think?"

Whether she believed me or not, Esther Kaplan bought in, and deferred some of her salary in the first few years in exchange for her partnership interest. The very next day, while Esther was running the office, I was buzzing about town, hustling for our $32 million.

✳

MOM'S LESSON #8: If you want to be in two places at once, borrow a reel-to-reel.

✳

THE LESSON LEARNED ABOUT DELEGATING

I realized that in trying to be everything to everybody at my fledgling company, I was only fooling myself.

I was going to have to put my confidence and wallet into someone else's hand and it scared me to death. In my heart, I knew no one else could run The Corcoran Group the way I could, so why, I reasoned, would I let someone try and maybe screw things up?

Deciding to share responsibility and control was the toughest move I ever had to make in building my business. But because of the way Esther was, it was also easy as pie. Right away, I saw a tremendous upside in being able to delegate the things I didn't like to do. I also saw that because Esther enjoyed those things, she might even do them better than I did. Good enough, anyway.

Once I'd decided Esther was the one to help me run things, I still had to convince her that it was a good idea. Why should she upset her own profitable apple cart for what might turn out to be pie in the sky?

So I shared my naïve dream with Esther, a big payday some Tuesday down the road for hamburgers today and every day for a while. When she didn't quite know what to make of that, I found a way of putting it in her own no-nonsense, very organized terms, laid out neatly in boxes, dollars, and cents. Then Esther could at least see that she liked where I was heading.

I made sure that Esther could maintain some of her sales income while helping me build our company. The arrangement enabled her to still meet her financial needs until "Tuesday" arrived. I didn't ask her to run the office full-time until the company's growth made it possible to make up the shortfall from her lost commissions.

We hit $32 million in commissions in fourteen years instead of the projected seven, and 500 salespeople made it happen rather than the 1,792 I'd projected. So, my projection was a bit off, but I know we would have accomplished it much later if I hadn't taken a leap of faith in hiring, and then promoting, Esther Kaplan.

WHO AND HOW TO HIRE

I've hired a lot of people since Esther Kaplan became the first vice president of The Corcoran Group, and I've learned a few things about how to pick 'em. The first thing to recognize is that while your goal may be to duplicate yourself, reel-to-reel, there's really no one quite like you. You've got to accept an imperfect copy.

What stops great leaders from hiring other people to lead is often their conviction that no one else can do the job as well as they can. And they're right to think that. But, sooner or later, if they're going to build a bigger business, they've still got to hire somebody to help them run things.

Here are my dozen tips for hiring great leaders:

1. **A job done 80 percent as well as you could do it is a job done well enough.**
   Forget about perfection; it doesn't exist.

2. **The speed of the boss is the speed of the team.**
   The boss sets the pace that everyone follows. If you don't lead by example, watch out.

3. **Leaders come in two flavors, expanders and containers.**
   The best leadership teams have a mix of both. Expanders, like me, are naturally inclined to make more and more of something. Containers, like Esther, are naturally inclined to keep everything in order. One without the other always runs into trouble, because after a great idea is birthed, it needs to be nursed.

4. **Always choose attitude over experience. Always.**
   People with the right attitude are a pleasure to work with. They are willing to learn, eager to try, and excited to discover something new. If someone likes to do things their way or no way, don't hire them. Bad attitude is bad news.

5. **All things being equal, always choose a woman over a man.**
   Women have more to prove than men, and they'll work much harder proving it. They work differently from men, their style is more collaborative, and they know how to read between the lines. Women are pragmatic, much more likely than men to tell the truth, and they're definitely more fun to work with. Besides, choosing a woman puts you on the cutting edge, since women are taking over anyway.

6. **Make sure they fit in.**
   A good organization is like a box of crayons. You need different colors of the spectrum, but all the crayons should fit in the box.

7. Make jobs for people, don't squeeze people into jobs.

Everyone has something they do best, and a manager's job is to find it and wrap a position around it. Esther Kaplan's purse indicated that she had the organizational flair to run a tight ship.

Most of the positions in my company were created *around* the specific people who hold them. Some examples:

- *Our Welcome Lady.* The beautiful young woman I found sitting behind the counter at my neighborhood florist had a smile I'd walk the extra four blocks to see. She was an anomaly, a *smiling New Yorker*! I hired her as a walkin', talkin' smile for our business. She warmly welcomes out-of-towners to our city and quickly introduces them to the right salespeople. Ours.

- *Our Swing Manager.* One of our talented salespeople spent half her time between appointments helping and coaching her colleagues, yet refused my offer to become a full-time sales manager. She said she had no interest in being tied down to "the twenty-four-hour-a-day, seven-days-a-week" routine of running an office. (And she was right, our sales managers never really had a peaceful day off.) We created a new position of "swing manager" around her. She got the flexibility she wanted, and the new position guaranteed our sales managers days off and carefree vacations.

- *Our Marketing Coach.* There's always a day when a great salesperson decides he or she "doesn't want to be in sales anymore." So, when one of our best salespeople and self-promoters made that declaration, I handed him a paintbrush and told him to paint a picture of his dream job. The picture he painted was one of teaching other people how best to market themselves to get more business. He's now our in-house guru on self-promotion and a singular attraction in luring good salespeople from other firms.

8. Make sure people see their gift.

It's the manager's job to find the gift and underline it. Just like my mother identified the gifts in her children, a good manager helps people see their potential and reminds them of it regularly.

9. Tell them to make mistakes. Make it part of their job.

Failing and growing are the same thing, and a good manager communicates that belief. I've found that sharing my own failures is the surefire way to put failure in the positive light it deserves. It's no good if people are afraid to fail, or afraid to tell you they've failed. That atmosphere leads to a lot of skeletons stashed in closets. It's not fun when they start spilling out—and they always do.

10. Throw them the ball and cut the string.

Make sure people understand that they don't need to report each day's progress. But make sure they also understand that you expect to hear from them whenever they get stalled.

I've found that the more confidence you express in people, the harder and more creatively they will work to solve a problem. When you tell someone, "You're a bright woman, you'll figure it out," the last thing in the world she wants is to come back and say, "I can't do it."

11. Never step in front of those you hire.

The boss's place is in the background, getting behind people and lending them support. Once you promote someone to a position of authority, the worst thing you could do is make a decision for her, or let her subordinates go around her to get to you. All too often a boss will let longtime subordinates make an "end run" around the new manager, completely undermining that person's chance to lead effectively.

12. Become a grandparent to your young leaders, not a nervous parent.

Thank them, bless them, pray for them, and spoil them. But don't day-to-day control them. Instead, give them an emotional massage every day, just like the back rubs Nana gave us at bedtime, as she whispered sweetness into our ears.

SIX WAYS TO MOTIVATE

1. Identify someone's hot button, the thing that motivates them.

Just asking, "What would make your job a dream come true?" will yield amazingly attainable answers. Individual hot buttons can run the gamut from financial stability to status, authority, creative expression, or just a comfortable desk chair. But everyone has at least one motivational hot button.

Esther was interested in respect and financial security. The position of first vice president gave her the respect she needed. Each time I sought her counsel on important decisions, her pride was enhanced. She was in charge of the company's money and that made her feel financially secure.

Zero in on someone's hot button, and wrap that person's position around it. By understanding their personal goals, they're able to achieve their professional happiness.

2. Let them name their own price.

Negotiating a price for your own labor is an unnerving experience for everyone. Even the most confident people will second-guess themselves after agreeing on their compensation. When deciding upon the right compensation for a position, ask the person to structure their own compensation package, and then pay them a little bit more. I've always found that people name a lower price than I would have given if I had suggested their compensation. Also, paying people just a little bit more than they've asked for is the best shortcut I know to long-term love and loyalty.

3. **Give a bonus instead of a raise.**

No matter how much a raise is appreciated, it's soon taken for granted. An unexpected bonus, on the other hand, leaves a sweet, satisfying aftertaste long after the money is spent. In fact, a well-placed bonus conditions the receiver to make extra efforts to say thanks and motivates them to work even harder for the next one.

4. **Little kindnesses are the sure road to loyalty.**

Nothing is more corporate or less effective than public displays of the boss's appreciation. Grandstanding only serves the guy on the grandstand, and everybody knows it. Instead, express your appreciation one-on-one and let the recipient share your compliment with everyone else.

5. **Share your dream.**

Show people why and how their role is essential to your dream. By sharing your dream, you speak to people's souls and allow them to be part of it.

6. **Guard your gold.**

Remember that gold shines. After you've molded a great new leader, your competitors will try to poach her. So be darn sure you've already made your leader loyal.

9

It's Your Game,
Make Up Your Own Rules

1981. Suffern, New York.

The *New York Times* headline read:

NEW YORK REAL ESTATE MARKET
SHOWS SIGNS OF LEVELING OFF

"According to Brewster Ives," the article read, "chairman of the Douglas Elliman, Gibbons & Ives Real Estate Company, Manhattan home prices have dipped for the first time since 1973 . . ."

"*Blah, blah, blah . . .*" I said to myself as I scratched out my competitor's name in the *New York Times* with my black Magic Marker.

"Damn! Why is that guy always in the paper and I'm not?" I complained to the man seated next to me at the industry gathering at the Holiday Inn in Suffern, New York.

"You probably need a PR guy," he grinned.

"A P-what guy?"

"A public relations company," he said, spreading his fingers in a broad wave. "And, hi, I'm Bill Higgins from Higgins Realtors in New Jersey. We're the oldest and boldest real estate company in the state, and I suppose you're the new broker from the city?" He didn't wait for my response. "I heard this PR guy speak at a conference last month in Boston, named Solomon—Steve Solomon. He's from Manhattan and that's what he does, gets people in the paper. You should look him up. He got my name on the front page of the *Bergen Record,*" Higgins bragged. "Yep, right under Nancy Reagan!"

My immediate reaction was *Who is this guy? And what the heck is he talking about?* But when I returned to the city, I called Steve Solomon. The game of PR was about to begin.

"You charge *seven hundred and fifty dollars a month! Every* month?" I asked in disbelief, whisking my blond bangs away from my eyes. "Mr. Solomon, that's an awful lot of money; it's more than I'm spending on all our advertising!" My palms were sweating. I stood up to straighten the seams on my new red dress, and paced once around my chair before sitting back down.

Steve Solomon, a dark-suited, serious man with a thoughtful face, explained, "The best way to make your company known is to put out some sort of survey or report on the marketplace. Something with a lot of numbers—the media love numbers. Maybe compare this year's prices to last year's."

"I guess that makes sense," I said without a clue as to how or where I was going to get $750. "Could we call it something important like the *New York City Apartment Price Report?*"

"Maybe," he considered diplomatically, jotting a few words in his notebook. "Or how about calling it *The Corcoran Group Report,* or, even better, *The Corcoran Report.*"

"*The Corcoran Report?*" I paused and listened to the sound of that. "But it doesn't mean anything," I said. "No one knows who or what Corcoran is."

"No," he answered, "but do the report and they will."

Summer. Undercliff Avenue.

My hands were covered with chalk as I finished my masterpiece, "The Largest Sidewalk Snail Game in the History of the World!" The Snail wriggled up and down the sidewalk, over the curb, and onto Undercliff Avenue. It stretched from Mrs. Rinebold's house, past Mrs. Gibbons', and right up our front steps.

Square after square of symbols and shapes showed the neighborhood kids exactly what to do as they hopped onto each space: first with two feet, then one right foot, and the next commanding a left foot in reverse. Next came one of my tricky spirals I called "spinners," followed by a dozen other variations on and on to the end.

The kids began lining up for their turn to hop, clap, jump, and spin their way around to the finish line.

As usual, Mean Michael Mertz was standing at the head of the line. He darted through the first ten squares, pretending to almost trip on the reverse double spin, then bolted through the last forty spaces, making my Snail look easy.

Fatty Patty stepped up next, and I just knew he was going to hurt himself. There was no way his chubby legs could possibly do my double spinner.

"Wait a minute, Patty!" I said, grabbing my pink chalk and walking over to the square. "I gotta fix one thing." I erased the spinner with the sole of my sneaker, drew two new feet in the same square, and stood up. "Okay, go ahead, Patty."

"*No way!*" Michael Mertz protested loudly. "You can't do that! You can't just go and change it like that!"

"Oh yes she can," Ellen said, defending me.

"No way, no how!" he repeated. "*You can't do that!*"

All the kids began shouting. It was Timmy Tom who broke the impasse when he peeped, "Why don't we ask Mrs. Corcoran, because *she's the mother.*"

I ran up the steps and through the side alley into the kitchen. Mom was at the ironing board.

"Mom!" I blurted, trying to catch my breath. "Michael Mertz says I can't change a square in my Snail game. Can I?"

"It's your game, Barbara Ann," she said, rendering her decision without lifting her eyes off Dad's white shirt, "So make up your own rules."

I bounded down the stairs, shouting Mom's verdict: *"My mother says it's my game and I can make up my own rules!"*

I stepped off the curb and stared Michael in the face. "And my rules are: It's *Patty's* turn!"

Fatty Patty finished the game on two solid feet, and I promised myself that tomorrow I'd make my Snail even bigger! I'd start all the way up at the library, come down past the church, and wind my Snail right back up Oxen Hill clear out of Edgewater!

July 1981. The Corcoran Group.

I slid a piece of our new Corcoran Group stationery into my Selectric, still thinking about the blank sidewalks of Undercliff Avenue and how I filled them with my Snail games. I stared at the blank page and scrolled up. I knew I had little to work with now, but it was my game, and I was going to make up the rules.

The only information I had gathered for *The Corcoran Report* was a list of our apartment sales over the last six months, exactly eleven. So, I added up all the sale prices and divided by eleven. I checked it twice and the answer was $254,232. I rounded the figure up to an even $255,000 and typed in the words "AVERAGE APARTMENT PRICE" next to it.

"There!" I said, surprising myself. "That was pretty easy and the average price seems about right."

I was feeling smart and started thinking that a *price per room* might also be useful! So, I sat back and pictured all the apartments I had shown over the last few months and how many rooms each one had. I was writing fast and knew that the algebra I had repeated twice in summer school was going to come in handy.

So, let's see, I pondered, as I riffled through the stack of listing forms. *It looks like there are a lot more one-bedrooms than two-bedrooms, and a few more two-bedrooms than three-bedrooms. And since one-bedroom apartments have three or three and one half rooms, and two-bedrooms have four or four and one half rooms, and three-bedrooms have either five, six, or seven rooms, then,* I thought as I massaged my exploding head, *the average apartment in Manhattan must have about four and one quarter rooms!* "Yep, that's it," I decided aloud, and began to type.

ƆG

THE CORCORAN REPORT
1981 MID-YEAR STUDY

"An in-depth 6-month Survey and Analysis of Conditions and Trends in the New York City Luxury Apartment Marketplace."

AVERAGE APARTMENT PRICE: $255,000*

AVERAGE ROOM PRICE: $57,000*

*rounded up to the nearest thousand dollars

For press inquiries contact:
Barbara Corcoran,
President, The Corcoran Group
212-355-3550

I yanked *The Corcoran Report* from the typewriter, made Xerox copies, and mailed one to every reporter who had written an article in that Tuesday's *New York Times.* I even included the sportswriters, figuring that one of them might know somebody rich like Joe Namath who might be looking to buy a big apartment.

Sunday, August 30, 1981. New York Times.

The headline read:

STUDY SHOWS CO-OP PRICES NEARLY QUINTUPLED

I stared at the headline in absolute disbelief. The story read: "According to Barbara Corcoran, president of The Corcoran Group Real Estate Company, the average price . . . has reached an all-time high of $255,000 . . ."

I read the line again slowly, and then once more out loud. I put the *Times* back down on my desk and thought, *I must be in the middle of some kind of Catholic miracle!*

I took out the black-handled scissors from my drawer and carefully cut out the words "According to Barbara Corcoran, president of The Corcoran Group Real Estate Company." I coated the paper with some Cutex nail hardener, blew it dry, and taped it above the rotary dial on my phone.

✳

MOM'S LESSON #9: It's your game, make up your own rules.

✳

THE LESSON LEARNED
ABOUT BECOMING A SOMEBODY

The *New York Times* story put me square in the middle of the Manhattan real estate game, playing it by my own rules.

Two weeks after the release of our first *Corcoran Report*, I overheard one of my salespeople pitching for a listing on the phone. "I'm calling from The Corcoran Group," he said to the potential seller. "Let me spell it for you. It's C-O-R-C— Oh, you've *heard* of us?!"

Unlike advertising, publicity has the power of the third-party endorsement. And advertising could never buy me the credibility of being quoted in that Sunday's *New York Times*.

Writers need numbers and statistics to substantiate their stories. That makes numbers the slam dunk of all good publicity. Since co-op sale prices were considered private and never published, my numbers were as good as anyone else's—maybe even better.

HOW TO MAKE A STATISTICAL REPORT THAT GETS NOTICED

1. Don't follow rules that don't exist.

I had shown enough apartments over the preceding seven years to come to a *reasonable* conclusion about the size of a typical Manhattan apartment. Although our eleven sales might not have been enough to provide a solid basis for an industry average, they didn't have to be. They just had to be *believable* for the marketplace.

I had as much right to be in the game as anyone else, and by positioning myself as an authority, I became the authority.

2. Keep the report simple and name it after your business.

Our first *Corcoran Report* was one page long and had one good hook—sale prices. And since everyone was interested in knowing what the next guy was paying for his apartment, we told them. Besides, it's a lot easier to churn out a simple statistical report than invent a new story every month.

3. Be consistent.

Many of my competitors soon copied our market report, but they were never consistent in publishing it. *The Corcoran Report* came out *every* six months, rain or shine. And reporters learned to rely on it.

4. Always tell the truth.

In the media world, honesty is the key to longevity and there are three good reasons to tell it like it is, even when it seems to be against your best business interests. First, bad news *always* prints. And when the market is bad and you have little money for advertising, that's just when you need free publicity most. Next, when you're willing to speak the truth on how bad things really are, reporters learn to trust you. Later, when you announce a market recovery, they believe you. Last, reporting bad news won't fuel a business downturn. Contrary to common belief, it simply labels it and gets it over with.

5. Ignore the naysayers.

When I issued our first *Corcoran Report*, our most dedicated salespeople argued vehemently against it. They believed that eleven sales were not enough to produce an average price and feared we could lose our credibility. What they didn't realize was that we had no credibility. We had nothing to lose and nowhere to go but up.

P.S. Seven years later, I married Bill Higgins, the guy who first told me about public relations. He's still impossible to understand, but, boy, is he smart.

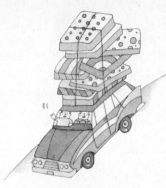

10

There's Always Room
for One More

1981. New York City.

Esther walked into my office and quietly closed the glass door behind her. She was now hiring and training our salespeople, helping manage the office, and keeping our finances in check. In short, she was doing everything I had no time to do, and making it possible for me to continue bringing in new business.

"Well?" I asked as she sat down after her latest round of interviews. "How were they?"

"I'd say that out of the bunch, the last two candidates were fairly good," Esther replied, tilting her head slightly to the left. "But, Barbara . . ." By now I knew that any time Esther's head tilted to the left and she said, "But, Barbara," her left brain was going into overdrive. She went on, "With every desk filled and every salesperson productive and not an inch of space for a new desk anywhere, *why*, might I ask, are we interviewing new salespeople?"

Spring. The front steps.

Mom came out of the screen door and leaned her broom against the house. *"Kids!"* she shouted, her belly protruding beneath her blue housedress, "Your dad will be coming down the hill any minute now with a *big* surprise!" We ran from the side yard to the front steps, each of us reaching our own conclusions about what the surprise might be. Mom stood on the top step with Baby Mary Jean on her hip, and we all sat beneath her and waited.

We heard Dad's green Rambler before we saw it. It clanked and growled like an old tanker. The used car salesman had told Dad the Rambler "operates *great* in low gear!" So Dad had kept it in low gear for the entire three years he'd owned it.

"Here he comes!" Mom shouted, pointing left up Library Hill. We watched as Dad made the turn off Edgewater Place with Uncle Bobby in the passenger seat beside him. They were honking and waving from beneath what looked like a mountain of six-foot boxes atop the car's roof. Piled at least five high, they were bouncing and flapping as Dad's Rambler came down Library Hill.

"Those suckers are moving!" Eddie yelled, as Dad waved excitedly and we all waved back. The boxed tower leaned dramatically to the left when Dad swerved to the right, and the Rambler screeched to a halt in front of our house.

"Avalanche!" Eddie yelled as ten twin mattresses thump-thump-thumped down the windshield and flipped onto the hood like dominoes. Uncle Bobby and Dad were still smiling and waving like beauty pageant winners on a wrecked float, their front doors webbed shut in clothesline.

Mom handed Mary Jean off to Denise and bounded down the steps two at a time. She arched her back and put her hands squarely on her hips. *"Eddie!* You have *no* common sense. *None!* Why didn't you tie the rope in *both* directions? I'm telling you, Ed, you're *just* like your father!"

"Sweetheart," Dad charmed with a smile as he leaned through the clotheslined window. "Couldn't you get a knife or something and help get us out of here?"

While Mom ran up for the knife, swearing she'd use it on Dad, we all stampeded down to get a better look at our new mattresses. Some of them had little red stripes, some had blue ones, and a few had small green polka dots. In a mad frenzy, we each staked a claim on our own mattress.

A mile of clothesline later, Dad and Uncle Bobby were cut out of the Rambler and they began taking the mattresses two at a time into our house.

Mom could always figure out a way to squeeze one more child into the boys' or girls' room. When Dad had told Mom that the Holy Angel's Academy for Girls was closing, she had immediately sent him to get ten of its best twin-size mattresses and then spent the morning mentally rearranging our beds toe-to-toe along each wall like railroad cars. Using her broom as a measuring stick to stake out each bed's space, Mom had calculated how to fit four beds into each room. As Dad and Uncle Bobby hoisted the mattresses into the house, she pointed out exactly where they were going.

"Girls' room!" she commanded, "against the right wall. Boys' room"—she pointed—"to the left of the closet." Dad and Uncle Bobby huffed and puffed and followed Mom's instructions until four twin-size beds were neatly arranged in each room. "Now, put the crib in the living room between the wall and the sofa," she finished, "and take the last two mattresses to the basement. We may end up needing them."

Esther sat with her hands neatly folded on her lap and her ankles crossed beneath her chair, primly waiting for my answer. "The reason we're interviewing salespeople, my dear Esther, is because I've figured out a way to add more desks," I said smugly. "Probably *thirty percent* more! It's the old 'toe-to-toe' routine, and I'll show you how it works."

I held up a manila folder on which I had drawn fourteen rectangles labeled "Desk," and fourteen small circles labeled "Chair." "Here's a picture of what we have now," I said. "Seven desks on the left side and seven on the right, all fourteen facing in the same direction, separated by the aisle in the middle."

Then, allowing the folder to drop open like a hatch door, I revealed my drawing on the other side. "*Voilà!*" I said. "And here's our same office with a total of *twenty* desks. Ten on the left, ten on the right, and the same aisle down the middle."

I pointed to my sketch and explained, "The key, you see, is the space *between* the desks. If we place the desks front to front, facing each other, we eliminate every third passageway behind the chairs, and it gives us three more desks on each side."

Esther studied the "After" drawing with suspicion and counted the rectangles and circles once more. "But will we still have the same eighteen inches for each chair to move back and forth?" she asked. I assured her we would, as we went out to measure the sales area.

I grabbed the office broom and turned it horizontally to measure the depth of a single desk including its chair. Then I clasped both hands on the broomstick to mark the measurement, and, turning the length of the broom back and forth, back and forth, I measured and counted off the imaginary desks as I went. The salespeople looked on, some smiling and others bewildered.

". . . eighteen, nineteen, twenty," I finished, and turned to Esther and said, "See? They'll fit. So let's hire those new people before someone else does!"

✳

MOM'S LESSON #10: There's always room for one more.

✳

THE LESSON LEARNED
ABOUT GROWING A BUSINESS

We expanded our company much like my parents expanded their family: When Mom announced, "Eddie, I'm pregnant!" Dad brought in another bed. The Corcoran Group grew from six sales-people to sixty in the first five years, and I learned that the secret to growing a business quickly is simply not waiting until you're "ready."

1. **Hire great people, and *then* worry about where to put them.**
   When I meet a great person I want to hire, I rarely have the room for them. But when the new person arrives, I always find a spot. We've divided a conference room four times to squeeze in more people, and I divided my own office twice.

   Finding a great new person is a lot like finding a beautiful new dress. If you buy the dress, you'll find a hanger to put it on.

2. **Open the next office *before* you're ready.**
   I always open my next office two years too early, while my competitors wait for the "right" time to expand. It's an easier ride to follow the pack into a proven territory, but it won't allow you to take the early lead and distance yourself from the rest.

   Common wisdom dictates that businesses often fail because they grow too fast and outstrip their cash flow. I have found that businesses get bigger faster when forced to run like hell to pump up their cash flow. Just as it's never really the right time to have a baby, it's never really the right time to open your next office. For me, *now* always proved to be the best time.

3. **Move into a space much bigger than you need.**
   Moving into a bigger space is the equivalent of putting a gun to your own head. It forces you to move faster, think quicker, and

find a way to pay the rent. With the enormous pressure of increased overhead, you're forced to double your business or die.

With every new office we opened, I made a habit of renting twice the space we actually needed. When I moved my first seven salespeople into an office with fourteen desks, I *had* to fill seven more.

In short, if you want to grow fast, put a gun to your head.

4. If they ask for a private office, give them a phone booth.
As New York rents climbed and office space grew tighter, our individual desk space shrunk from fifty-four inches to forty-eight inches to thirty-six inches per person. When our salespeople complained that our office had gotten too crowded and noisy, and their negotiations were no longer private, we answered their need for privacy by installing two free phone booths. The phone booths offered a quiet spot for personal calls and confidential negotiations, with the added benefit of less personal time wasted on the phone.

Private offices are no good for the sales business because a sales team's lifeblood is the free exchange of information. If you're tucked away in a private office, you're simply out of the loop. Also, privacy is expensive and one private office inevitably opens a Pandora's box of six other staff members wanting the same thing.

5. Share an office.
All good salespeople spend most of their time out of the office, leaving latitude for flexible desk arrangements. When offices are shared, information is exchanged and a lot less time gets wasted on memos, e-mails, and phone calls. Most of our top salespeople share offices with their assistants and/or other salespeople.

For years, I shared my office with Scott Durkin, my chief of staff. Hearing my conversations throughout the day enabled him to execute my orders while I was still on the phone promising them! Our shared space left absolutely no room for error, and made him such a quick judge of what needed doing that Scott is now the chief operating officer of the company.

6.   **Extend your territory beyond its natural borders.**
Every good boxer knows that if he's going to pack a powerful punch, the target's not the face, but a full foot behind the face. Business lies beyond every office wall, and to grab it, you need to reach beyond your physical space. Here's how our business was able to extend its reach:

- *Open houses in somebody else's house.* After we filled our conference rooms with sales desks and had no room to meet our customers at the office, we began to use our "apartments for sale" as satellite offices. We were the first company to publish specific property addresses in our Sunday "open house" advertisements, and, contrary to our competitors' dire predictions, it never led to muggings and thefts. Instead, we quadrupled the number of buyers responding to our ads and got to sit on some lovely settees in some of Park Avenue's most expensive homes.

- *A virtual office is virtually free.* With every inch of space filled and every salesperson productive, we still hired. Instead of a desk, we offered the new agents specialized training, access to our database, and business cards with the snappy new title of "virtual agent." As our virtual agents operated from their homes, we saved on office space, phone bills, paper clips, sodas, pens . . .

- *Referral directors (a.k.a. the ladies who lunch).* In the real estate business, the person who controls the property controls the marketplace, and finding a property to list is often a result of who you know. We widened our company's circle of influence beyond our sales force by establishing a second-string sales team called the "referral directors." These socially well-connected women introduced us to their friends, so we could secure the listings of their apartments and houses. In return, the referral directors got a commission, a real estate license, a business card, and part-time hours compatible with their very busy social agendas. Our prestige listings skyrocketed, and the referral fees were negligible when compared with the increased commissions.

7. **Use a big hook to catch a big fish.**
    Even though she had no interest in joining our company, I pursued a top-selling, high-end agent from another firm by making the unconventional offer that she could take 100 percent of her own commissions for the first year. I also offered to pay half the cost of a chauffeured Bentley. She said yes. By hiring her, our company stepped into the high-end market, and her car and driver became a moving billboard for luxury buyers. Over the next five years, the top salesperson from almost every one of my competitors joined our firm at our regular commission rate.

We often set boundaries on ourselves and cause bottlenecks that cost money.

Every business can hire more people, open new offices, and lease bigger spaces before it's ready. It's the only formula I know for aggressive growth.

11

Go Play Outside

Winter 1982. New York City.

The New York real estate market was exploding and apartment prices were ballooning by the week. A new phenomenon called overbidding had just begun, adding another layer of stress on top of the already stressed-out sales environment. It seemed everyone in New York was making money, and had decided all at once to spend it on real estate. Everyone wanted New York, and my salespeople were totally exhausted.

I jumped in a cab on the way to my next afternoon showing, my thoughts bouncing between how I would get my next customer to make a high-enough bid on the one hand, and how I'd get my salespeople to take a needed break on the other. At our Monday sales meeting, I had once again suggested that everyone plan some vacation time, but from the glazed response on everyone's face, I figured it wasn't likely to happen.

As my cab turned the corner onto Riverside Drive, I decided I'd better plan a vacation for them.

Winter. The side yard.

"Snow day!" Mom shouted from the living room.

Nothing could compare to the mornings we'd wake up and hear Mom's rare pronouncement of those most spectacular words. "Snow day" meant "no school."

We popped out of our beds, jumped into our play clothes, and headed for the front radiator, where Mom had already set up her snow day station. Our gloves were already toasting on top of the radiator with our rubber boots warming below. By the front door, Mom had lined up old cardboard boxes, her biggest cookie pans, a trash can lid, and anything else she could dig out of the basement or kitchen that could serve as a sled. We put on our boots, gloves, and mittens, grabbed a "sled," and Mom gave us the once-over before pushing us out the door with her usual "Go play outside!"

Minutes before frostbite set in, we'd rush back in to the radiator's warmth where Mom, like a pit crew in a car race, got us in and out in thirty seconds flat. She yanked off our wet gloves and tossed them on top of the radiator to dry, giving each of us a pair of dry socks to put on our hands. She pulled off our boots, replaced our wet socks with dry ones, and sent us back outside. By day's end, the sock drawer was empty.

As traffic couldn't make it up or down River Road, Dad had the day off, too. Mom handed him Mary Jean and said, "Ed, take a dishpan and fill it with snow for Tommy. He's feverish, and I'll help him make snowballs inside."

After taking Tommy a dishpan of snow, Dad packed a snowdrift hard against the front retaining wall that separated our yard from the sidewalk. He dragged his two-story wooden ladder up to the very end of our backyard, the part that merged into the cliff behind our house.

"HEY, KIDS!" Dad yelled down, holding the ladder in place against the hill. "Hop on!"

We all raced to the top of the hill. "I call front!" Marty shouted, getting there first and taking the lead rung. The rest of us climbed on behind, locking our heels onto the wooden rungs.

"Oh, *no*, you don't!" Eddie declared, pushing Marty off the ladder into the snow. "I'm the oldest, so *I* get the front."

Marty sprang up in a flash and reached back toward Eddie, his fist cocked. "Cut it out, boys!" Dad commanded. "Marty, either get on the ladder and have some fun, or we're leaving without you." Marty pouted into place on a middle rung. "Ready!?" Dad hollered, as we all stared downhill, clenching the side rails with our hands.

"Yes!" we yelled in unison. Dad jostled the ladder side to side as though he were losing control.

"Are you *sure* you're ready?" he taunted.

"Yes. Oh yes!" we pleaded back, overwhelmed with anticipation.

"Then get going!" And with a quick shove, Dad jumped on the back of the ladder and sent it lunging forward, zero to sixty in less than a second!

We screamed a Palisade's Amusement Park scream as we zipped through the side yard, hurtling down toward Undercliff Avenue. We were picking up speed as we sailed toward the six-foot cinder-block retaining wall at the bottom. The front riders shrieked as their half of the ladder went airborne and momentarily waited for the back half to catch up.

Then, all at once, we shot off the ledge, sailed over the sidewalk, and thumped down squarely in the middle of the street, just behind a lone passing car that was sliding its way down Undercliff Avenue. We lay in the street, a jumbled pile of kids laughing until our sides and faces hurt.

Eddie offered Marty his hand and pulled him up. "Okay, Marty, you go first this time," he said, and, still laughing, Eddie and Marty helped Dad lug the ladder back up the hill.

Mom was changing the sheets in the girls' room when she spotted us flying by the side window. It was our third trip on Dad's death-defying ladder, and John caught a quick glimpse of Mom from the front rung. "It's Mom!" he gasped and pointed, as we plummeted toward the wall.

By the time we hit the street, Mom had barreled through the house, was down the steps, and had her face within two inches of Dad's. I noticed her blue slippers were soaked and, from what I could see, she looked cold and she sure looked angry. "Eddie!" she screamed. "Eddie, you have no common sense, absolutely none! Get the kids off the ladder NOW before you kill them," she seethed, "or I swear, Eddie, I'll kill you!"

We cupped our socked hands over our mouths to choke back our laughter, until Dad leaked out his Cheshire cat smile. When we all exploded into a fit of laughter, even Mom began to laugh, and we knew for sure we had the best family in town.

1982. Snow day. Whaley Lake.

"*Ice-skating?!*" Esther repeated. "But I don't know *how* to skate!"

"That's just it," I told her. "*Nobody* does. But *everybody* will when they get there!"

I had just bought my first house, for $75,000, a nine-room fixer-upper on Whaley Lake in Dutchess County. The house had six bedrooms, six bathrooms, two cabanas, two boathouses, and absolutely no land. My purchase was the classic case of buying "the biggest house on the worst block." Twelve years later, I would sell it for . . . $75,000.

"I have the whole weekend figured out, Esther," I continued, explaining my plans for our first company retreat. "I bought twenty pairs of ice skates for everyone, all in different sizes: white ones for the ladies and some black ones for the men. I also bought four sleds, eight sleeping bags for those who won't get beds, and twenty pairs of cheap wool mittens."

"*Cheap?*" Esther interrupted. "Nothing about this sounds cheap to me."

I dismissed Esther's look of concern with a quick wave of my hand, and continued, "And I've talked my brother Tee into catering the whole weekend!"

"Tee? But isn't that brother a cabdriver?" she asked with growing concern.

"Yeah, but he got his weekend shift covered and he's bringing Judy Somebody, one of the other cabdrivers, and he says she's a really good cook." Esther tilted her head.

"It'll all work out just fine," I went on. "And I got a great deal on a school bus to take everybody up on Friday night. We'll leave here around seven, and when we get there, the table will already be elegantly set, the flowers arranged, a fire burning, and a luscious meal will await us." I waited to see if Esther could picture it. "And after a great night's sleep, we'll all get up, eat a big breakfast, and have all day Saturday for ice-skating—and all day Sunday, too! We'll leave on Sunday around six and be back to the city no later than eight, eight-thirty the latest."

Esther looked pale.

We opened our eyes Saturday morning to a crisp, icy-cold day. The night before had been just perfect. The bus showed up on time, the dinner was truly gourmet, and while we ate and drank, we talked about what our office needed, what we all wanted, and what we all dreamed about doing together. We came up with a flurry of new ideas, so I grabbed a piece of junk mail and jotted them down. I starred someone's idea to produce a *Corcoran Report* strictly on new condominium prices. I liked it because we had never sold a condominium and I wanted to get into that market. Then, like kids at a giant slumber party, we climbed into our beds and sleeping bags and fell asleep.

By 9:00 A.M. on Saturday, we had finished breakfast and were all sitting on the boathouse ledge, juggling sizes and putting on our skates. Despite her inhibitions, Esther laced up first and desperately clung to the boathouse wall.

"You look like a natural over there, Esther," I joked, and chinned in her direction. "Now, hurry up, everybody, we don't want to keep Dorothy Hamill waiting!"

Although this would be my first skate on Whaley Lake, it sure looked like the kind of lake you'd want to skate on. It was one mile long, a half mile wide, and frozen over as far as I could see.

Ron Rossi, our leading salesperson, glided out onto the ice. He was resplendent in a one-piece Bogner snowsuit with matching chartreuse gloves. His ensemble's finishing touch was a long magenta and yellow Hermès scarf, which floated behind him as he pushed off the boathouse wall. In a previous life, Ron had been a world champion ballroom dancer, and from the looks of his first spin, we suspected he had been on the ice before.

"Follow Ron!" I gushed, and like ducklings doing their first waddle, we all got behind Ron as he demonstrated a large figure eight. After a few hundred falls, Ron had us looping large figure eights back and forth, back and forth, farther and farther out onto the ice. Esther stayed behind practicing her glide close to shore.

We were almost to the middle of the lake when I noticed we had attracted an audience on the shore. Squinting my eyes against the sun, I recognized the man in front of the old Gloyde's Motel as Old Man Gloyde himself. He was waving to us, and I waved back with enthusiasm. He shouted, "That's *n i c e*, that's *n i c e!*"

"*T h a n k s!*" I acknowledged in the loudest voice I could muster. "*W a t c h   t h i s!*" And with a quick tap of my right toe, I turned my left foot and went into my best amateur version of a twirl. I made a point of holding my hands straight out with pinkies up, just like Ron had taught us.

Mr. Gloyde seemed to like my twirl because he waved even more vigorously, yelling again, "That's *n i c e*, that's *n i c e!*"

I was thinking about attempting a pretty pirouette, when I noticed Esther standing up on the boathouse ledge. She was waving just like Mr. Gloyde. When I heard the ice creak and begin to moan, it hit me. "Nice" wasn't "nice"—it was "ice." "Thin *i c e!* Thin *i c e!*" And we were skating on it!

"Let's get the *hell* out of here!" I screamed, and the entire Corcoran Group shrieked in unison as the ice under our skates began to crack. Our panicked feet raced toward the shore, every man for himself, as the splitting ice chased us from behind. What could have only been two minutes at the most felt like a ten-mile run.

We all groped at Esther's legs as we clambered up onto the boathouse floor. We were huffing and puffing from our near-death experience. "You okay? You okay? You okay?" we chorused, as we scanned each other's faces. I looked around at my nineteen exhausted speed skaters, pulled off my hat, and started to laugh. With that, the whole boathouse rocked with laughter and I knew we had just become the best team in town.

※

MOM'S LESSON #11: Go play outside.

DAD'S BEST LESSON: Fun is fun.

※

THE LESSON LEARNED
ABOUT HAVING FUN

Conducting business as usual always results in usual business, but playing together creates extraordinary business.

Our weekend away at Whaley Lake not only built cohesiveness, it also made a community out of twenty vastly different personalities, and I instantly recognized that if we continued to play together, we could become the strongest company in town.

This is what I've learned about having fun:

1. **Happy people work better.**
   It's hard to leave good feelings back on the playing field. Inevitably, they find their way back to the office.

2. **Fun makes people laugh, and you can't help but like someone who's laughing.**
   People like each other better while they're playing. Playing together unites differences and breaks down barriers between people. It's also the best cleanser for bad feelings, old grudges, and ill will.

3. **Only in the context of fun do people get the chance to see their colleagues beyond their usual work roles.**
   Fun lets people get to know their colleagues better, learn about their families, their kids, and where they're from. By socializing, people discover other common grounds beyond the workplace.

4. **Playing is the best way to bring rivals together.**
   Strong salespeople are free agents, independent by nature, and often don't naturally make good teammates. But allow two rivals to vent their competitiveness in a spirited game, and they become a team.

5. **If you want good ideas for the office, go play outside.**

All of our best new business ideas were thought of while outside the office—our advertising campaigns, our publicity ideas, office perks, and whole new ways of doing business. The things we discovered while playing outside were all brought back to the office, like free massages and manicures, free soft drink coolers, Ping-Pong tables, and yoga classes. Playing outside always offers a fresh perspective and always stimulates new ideas.

TIPS FOR PLANNING GOOD FUN

1. **Play on company time.**

Most salespeople subscribe to the "Make it while you can" philosophy and run themselves ragged trying to do so. Planning for fun during company time gives the salespeople permission to take a day off and to do it without guilt.

One of our most successful annual sales meetings was scheduled to last three hours. But ten minutes into the meeting, I surprised everyone by inviting them next door into a private movie theater where together we watched the inspiring movie *Pay It Forward*.

Even our management retreats are scheduled during the workweek. They get three days away from the office at a luxury resort, and they come home with a tan, deepened friendships, renewed energy, and new ideas for the business. And while they're away, we're able to discover new management talent because other salespeople step up to the plate acting as substitute managers.

2. **Surprise them!**

Our company quickly outgrew the sleepovers at the Whaley Lake house. When I bought the next house, the smallest house on the best block with a lot of land, we began to bus two hundred, three hundred, then four hundred people up for mid-week picnics. At our first picnic, there was a sixty-foot hot-air balloon waiting in the backyard to give everyone a ride. We formed cheering and rescue squads when we faked a few problems in getting the balloon back down. Our salespeople had the same thrill as we did as kids when my dad jostled the wooden ladder beneath us on top of the hill.

One year, a five-thousand-pound elephant and a spitting camel waited on the front lawn to give safari rides, and yet another year, we leased ten Thoroughbreds in full gear and everyone got to run them up and down the back fields.

Perhaps the best surprise was the year everyone arrived to find that there was no surprise! An hour later, with hundreds of people picnicking on blue-checked blankets, a motorcycle gang of tattooed guys dressed in black leather and chains roared up onto the lawn, revving their engines and circling the frightened crowd. I jumped up and indignantly shouted, "You're on private property! Leave or I swear I'll call the police!" As someone ran to call 911, one of the bikers removed his helmet and revealed that "he" was really a "she" with a big smile, bright blue eyes, and long blond hair. The gang turned out to be my sister Mary Jean and her born-again Christian motorcycle club that came all the way from Pennsylvania to "crash" our party.

"So," I asked my shocked guests, "who wants a ride?"

3. People most resistant to fun need it the most.

People sometimes resist fun simply because they've never had it. All they need is a little encouragement. Our most proper Park Avenue ladies were the first to hike up their skirts and hop on the back of the Harley-Davidsons. They blissfully roared up and down the back roads, clutching their pearls as tight as they held on to the drivers.

4. Change keeps fun fresh.

When our company outgrew picnics at my house, we invented
new ways to keep the party going. Instead of corporate Christmas parties, we began a tradition of "February Sweetheart Parties." In real estate, as in many other businesses, February is the
slowest, most depressing month of the year, and it's the month
when people need to party the most. Also, since few parties are
planned in February, the best places in town are available at the
cheapest rates.

5. Themes make teams.

Our first black-tie Sweetheart Party took place in an abandoned
warehouse in Queens. My guests' adrenaline started pumping
when they were greeted by a huge man holding a gun in the
graffiti-covered industrial elevator. The elevator opened into a
ten-thousand-square-foot warehouse my brother Tee (cabdriver
turned caterer) had transformed into a speakeasy.

Every year, people eagerly look forward to the announcement of the February party's theme. When the theme was "Diva
or Drag," men and women cross-dressed for the occasion and
laughed about it for months to come. We held our "Stars on
Broadway" party in a theater on Forty-second Street, and a few
days before the party, we took our managers to rummage
through the city's largest costume shop in search of perfect star
costumes. Our wardrobe outing turned out to be a party in itself.
The moment I opened the party as Carol Channing lip-synching
"Hello, Dolly," the party was a success.

When the theme was "The Glamorous Forties," I tromped
through every costume shop in New York trying on and rejecting
a series of 1940s ball gowns because they were just what people
expected me to wear. Still without an outfit on the morning of
the party, I spotted a cardboard box marked "Girdles" in a
Greenwich Village drag queen shop. Five hours later, I walked

into the glamorous Rainbow Room high atop Rockefeller Plaza wearing a 1940s girdle and 46-double-D bra stuffed with two softballs, seam stockings, and an ice pack pinned to my head. As a "1940s woman with a morning-after hangover," I was the belle of the ball.

6. **Fun always follows the leader.**

In my 1940s costume, I got more kisses and gropes from my salespeople and employees than I got in the last ten years of my marriage. My insanity made the gossip columns, and, most important, I made a big deposit in our company loyalty bank simply because I was smart enough to be stupid.

7. **Make the party a madman's plan.**

Fun isn't logical. Fun happens when you take people out of their normal routine and drop them into an abnormal circumstance. When I'm dreaming up a new fun idea, I think of myself as a half-mad scientist in a well-stocked laboratory mixing up the potions. I take a little of this and a little of that and try to create something entirely new.

8. **Take a few chances.**

I've often been surprised by what happened during company fun, but I've never been disappointed. Making real fun is a cross between good planning and taking a leap of faith. Taking the leap of faith creates the spontaneity that the best things happen. When my brother Tee and his cabby friend Judy cooked for our first ice-skating party, their delicious food and amazing presentation gave birth to a successful new catering business. The chances were much better that their food would be a disaster rather than be exceptional. But it proved that harebrained schemes often lead to great discoveries.

9. Snap some pictures.

You double the pleasure of company playtime by taking pictures. A photo is nothing short of an everlasting echo of a really good time, and proof that, yes, the boss did come to the party wearing only a girdle.

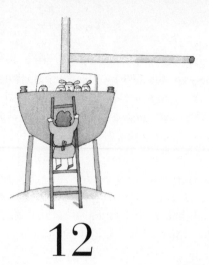

12

When the Clubhouse Is Quiet, They're Probably Not Making Spaghetti

Summer. Mrs. Harrison's backyard.

We found Charlie's boat wedged inside the big chicken shed in Mrs. Harrison's backyard. The Harrisons lived three doors up in a house almost identical to ours. But rather than having three families on three floors, Mrs. Harrison only had three kids and rented the rest of her rooms to eight old men.

The great thing about the chicken shed was its roof. It was the only place from which we could reach Old Maid Stella's cherry tree. Stella's tree hung high over her fence, leaving countless juicy cherries dangling just out of reach above our heads in the Harrison yard. But we could climb onto the shed's roof, shimmy over to the edge, and pick a handful of cherries. Stella's third-floor window looked onto the roof and she was always peeking out trying to catch us stealing her cherries.

"*Aaaaahh!*" Skinny Timmy Tom Harrison screamed one hot afternoon. "It's Stella the Cherry Witch!" We all looked up to see

Stella's baggy, saggy eyes glaring at us from behind her chenille curtains. "She's got her broom! Run for your lives!" Stella opened the window and threw her broom at us like a javelin, and we took off across the tin roof. "Follow me!" Timmy Tom squawked, his skinny legs running ahead of him across the roof. Like a superhero, he leapt into the air, landing midway up the cliff that climbed dramatically behind the Harrison house.

"*Psst!* In here!" he beckoned, opening the tiny window in the old shed behind their house. I jumped off the roof with Kathy Harrison, Janet Cleary, Michael Mertz, and my brother Tee following. We scurried through the window and dropped into the cool, shadowy corner of the Harrisons' old shed.

We were huffing and puffing, our little hearts racing. "Oh, my gosh," I gulped leaning against the inside wall. "Did you see her eyes? They were glowing as red as her cherries!" A few beams of light streaked through the windows, splashing light over the contents of the shed. "What's *that?*" I gasped at the giant hulking structure looming above us, twice as tall as any of our heads.

"That's Charlie's boat," Timmy Tom explained, "He's been building it in here with his own hands since I was three. He said he's gonna sail away on that boat."

"It's beautiful!" Janet Cleary gushed as she caressed the bottom of the boat, feeling its smooth, shiny wood. The boat ran from one end of the shed to the other.

"Hey, let's get in," I said, already climbing the ladder.

"Be careful!" Michael Mertz warned. "It might be dangerous."

"Are you a *scaredy cat*, Michael Mertz?" I taunted.

"I'm not scared of nothing," he said, following me up.

One by one we climbed up the ladder onto the deck of Charlie's boat and then stepped down below into its cabin. Though unfinished, the boat was already outfitted with tin kitchenware and two blue blankets. "This will be our new clubhouse!" I declared. It was clearly the greatest clubhouse in the world. "Who wants to join?" Everyone raised their hands. "It's our *secret* clubhouse," I said.

"Only us and no one else can know. Understand?" Everyone nodded their heads. "We'll have to seal the secret. Michael Mertz, you first."

"Whadda I gotta do, Barbara Ann?" he asked.

"Show us your heinie," I said. Without blinking, Michael Mertz dropped his pants, and as the light poured into the cabin of our new clubhouse, we all stared at Michael Mertz's little white eight-year-old behind.

After four more sets of cheeks were shown, I declared the first meeting of the "Showing Heinies Club" officially over.

"Tomorrow at noon," I whispered as we all climbed out of the boat, "and don't tell anyone, *not anyone!*" I felt I might be doing something wrong and figured with a mom like Mom, I didn't want to get caught.

On the fifth day of our Showing Heinies Club, five pairs of white cheeks were shining like harvest moons when the shed door swung open.

"It's Charlie!" I whispered, as we all squatted down, paralyzed and exposed.

"Who's up there?" Charlie hollered. "I know somebody's in there." The boat sat quiet, five naked behinds momentarily frozen in time. Then the boat rocked in its wooden cradle as all of us scrambled to pull up our pants. "Who's in there?" Charlie demanded.

I grabbed a metal plate and fork and banged a few of Charlie's tin Coleman pots around, trying to make as much noise as possible to disguise the sounds of snapping buttons and zipping zippers. "We're making spaghetti, Charlie," I shouted, "just making spaghetti."

One by one, five guilty faces popped over the edge of the boat and peered down at the old blond Swede. "It's just me," Timmy Tom peeped. "And me." "And me." "And me." "And me," the rest of the fanny five admitted.

"Making spaghetti, huh?" the old Swede said. "All right, but be careful in there. I'm going to sail away in that boat at the end of the summer."

On the eighth day of the Showing Heinies Club, we were right in the middle of Michael Mertz's turn when we heard my mom's voice outside the shed. "What are the kids doing in there, Charlie?" Mom asked. We all held our breath.

"Oh, they're fine, Mrs. Corcoran," he told her. "They're just making spaghetti."

"Nope, Charlie," she said. "When the clubhouse is quiet, they're *never* making spaghetti!" With that, she barged into our clubhouse, grabbed me and Kathy Harrison with one hand, told Michael to pull up his pants, and sent everybody home.

Summer 1983. Monday-morning meeting. The Corcoran Group.

We were right in the middle of a long, hot summer in New York. City streets and tempers alike steamed in the high temperatures. Our salespeople were happy to return to our air-conditioned office between showings, and this Monday morning they were all at their desks for our regular sales meeting, sipping the iced lemonade I had substituted for coffee. I took a deep breath, bracing myself to do what I had carefully planned to do.

Everyone at The Corcoran Group knew the company listing policy, which I had established at our first sales meeting. Our "share and share alike" policy required that salespeople post all new listings in our office files within one hour of getting the listing. Our policy was understood and welcomed, as it set us apart from the other firms' "every man for himself" practice. Their salespeople often pocketed special listings for their special customers, keeping them secret from the coworkers they viewed as competitors. In contrast, we shared our listings. At least, that was the idea.

Two summers earlier, Elaine had joined our company and quickly become our single best lister. She was French, quiet, and spent most of her time outside our office, rarely sharing a word with her associates. When she was in the office, her only activity was opening her middle drawer, exchanging papers from her brown leather briefcase, and scurrying out, her eyes darting from side to side.

Over the past month, Elaine's listing numbers had dwindled and in the last week, she had not added a single new listing to the company files. Paranoia was creeping into our happy group, and the warm "Hello" I had extended to Elaine that morning had been returned with a quick dart of her blue-eye-linered eyes to the left. I had had enough.

"Good morning, everyone!" I began as usual.

"Good morning, Barbara," the salespeople replied.

"Today I'd like to start our meeting by reviewing our listing policy," I said. "One of the differences between our firm and the others is that we share and share alike. We work hard and we play fair. I'd like to reiterate our policy that all new listings must be posted for everyone within one hour of getting the property. I want to remind everyone again that 'pocket listings' won't be tolerated. Does anyone have any new listings they want to put in the listing card files today?"

They shook their heads no, including Elaine.

"How about you, Elaine?" I asked as I walked over to her desk. "Would you have any listings to add to our company file today?"

"*Non,*" she replied.

"Okay," I said. "Would you mind opening your second drawer?"

"Nothing ees in dey're," she protested. "Juste old papers."

"You'll have to excuse me then, Elaine, while I look at your old files," I said, opening her drawer and removing the rubber-banded pile of papers, chock-full of listing information. I pulled out the top paper from the rest and read it aloud to the room: "Could anyone tell me if we have Apartment 4B at 60 Sutton Place South listed for $340,000?" Everyone shook their heads a tense, slow no. "It sounds nice," I continued. "It's a two-bedroom, two-bath with a terrace!"

"How about Apartment 12D at 1065 Park?" Again they signaled no. I quickly flipped through the thirty or so sheets, each with a different address. Then I confronted Elaine's bright eye-linered eyes and asked, "Elaine, is there any reason you haven't put these listings in our company files?"

Her lips quietly mouthed *"Non."*

"Pack your things," I leaned down and whispered into her ear. "And if you don't mind, I'll keep these."

We all watched as Elaine quickly shoved her desk accoutrements into her brown briefcase and huffed out of the office door.

The moment the door closed, the whole office erupted in cross-chatter, a mix of astonishment and relief. I took the pile of Elaine's papers and dealt them out like a blackjack dealer.

I had caught Elaine with her pants down and in the process charted a moral course for our company's future.

✳

MOM'S LESSON #12: When the clubhouse is quiet, they're probably *not* making spaghetti.

✳

THE LESSON LEARNED ABOUT SMELLING TROUBLE

My police action with Elaine that morning became folklore, and in the years that followed every new salesperson heard "The Tale of the Pocket Listing Lady."

When someone is uncharacteristically quiet you can be sure they are up to no good. They're either stirring up trouble, picking your pocket, or packing their bags. A manager's job is to speak up, shake up, and bring a troublemaker out of hiding. He'll manage to pull up his pants, if you knock on his door.

13

If You Want to Be a Cheerleader,
You Better Know the Cheers

⟡G

September 12, 1985

Dear Mr. Trump,

I thought you might like to see
this before I send it to the press.

Best regards,

Barbara Corcoran
President
The Corcoran Group

I clipped my note to The Corcoran Group's new *Top 10 Condo Report* and sealed the envelope. "Trump Tower," I said, handing it to the messenger, "the penthouse."

Donald Trump, who built a billion-dollar real estate empire with shameless self-promotion and sheer chutzpah, was the best-known businessman in the city and his name was synonymous with everything people both loved and hated about New York. Mr. Trump's latest enterprise was a sixty-eight-story black glass condominium next door to Tiffany's on the corner of Fifty-seventh and Fifth, where the old Bonwit Teller used to stand. He was billing his new "Trump Tower" as "The Most Expensive Address in the World." Only in New York could "most expensive" be a badge of honor, and The Donald wore it with pride. I wanted the "Corcoran Group" name to scream New York real estate as loudly as "Trump" did. And I had a plan.

Our *Top 10 Condo Report* didn't list Trump's trophy property in first place, second, or even third. The sales data I had collected relegated his highest-priced sale to fourth position behind Museum Tower, Olympic Tower, and The Galleria, Trump's main rivals in town.

Though I'd never met Mr. Trump, I knew my latest report would sizzle in his hands. Within an hour, he called me.

Cheerleading tryouts. High school.

I finished the Holy Rosary School in Edgewater as a charity "D" student. After my special reading class with Sister Stella Marie in second grade, school only got worse. After graduation from eighth grade, the Catholic kids with the good grades went to the Catholic high schools, while everybody else bused two towns over to the public school in Leonia.

I was shocked when an acceptance letter from St. Cecilia's Catholic High School arrived at the end of eighth grade. I thought they'd put the right slip in the wrong envelope. A chance at St. Cecilia's seemed like the first light at the end of a long, dark school tunnel. I promised my parents and myself that at my new school I would do a lot better.

On my first day at St. Cecilia's, the homeroom teacher asked me to be our student council representative. He picked me because

Corcoran started with *C*. I sat in the second seat behind Maureen Beckman, whose name started with a *B*, but she had already left when the bell rang. He handed me a list of questions to poll and collect the opinions of the other homeroom kids. The survey gave me the opening I needed to befriend my new classmates.

I was well on the road to popularity at St. Cecilia's when I flunked algebra, history, and Latin, and just as Dad warned, I was taking the bus up the hill for my sophomore year at the public high school in Leonia. I had blown my one chance to be somebody.

I looked up at the notice posted on the big bulletin board hanging outside the Leonia High School gym:

```
CHEERLEADER TRYOUTS
WEDNESDAY THRU FRIDAY
3 to 5 P.M.
IN THE GYM
```

It was obvious in my first two weeks at my new school that the popular girls were all from Leonia, not from Edgewater. And the *really* popular ones were the cheerleaders. They were pretty, they had nice clothes, and they were always surrounded by guys. They were everything I was not and wanted to be.

That's it! I said to myself looking at the poster. *I'm taking the fast road to popularity!* I printed my name on the sign-up sheet in the 4:45 Thursday spot.

I pushed open the heavy metal door of the large gym and realized it didn't look any bigger than the gym at St. Cecilia's. A cafeteria table was set up at the far end below the basketball hoop, and I noted the backboard above it said "AWAY." I thought it might be a bad sign.

Three women sat behind the table. I figured they were the judges. I recognized one as the gym teacher and guessed the other two women were probably teachers, too. Six cheerleaders were huddled in a sideline giggle, looking like burgundy-and-gold best friends. I clicked my way across the polished floor to center court. When the cheerleaders built a perfect pyramid, I panicked, wondering if I was expected to know how to build a pyramid, too.

"Name please," the gym teacher asked.

"Hi, I'm Barbara." I waved. "And I have an appointment for a four forty-five tryout."

"Yes, Miss Corcoran," the woman said, checking her clipboard. "Please remove your shoes." I took off my loafers, set them next to me, and faced the panel of judges in my stocking feet. I wished I had brought my sneakers.

Everyone turned their attention to me, including the pyramid, which quickly toppled and formed a perfect line to watch.

"Okay, then," the gym teacher said.

"Okay, what?" I asked.

"Let's see your cheer."

"What cheer?"

"Whichever cheer you choose."

That's when I realized I wasn't prepared. Not only did I not know a cheer, I hadn't ever even *seen* a Leonia cheer. I had to think fast. I figured the name they probably liked best was "Leonia." It was also the safest word for me to spell. So I spread my legs in an official cheerleader-type stance, puffed out my chest, shoved my fists into my hips, and began:

"Give me an *L!*" I shouted.

Silence.

"*L!*" I shouted back to myself, throwing my right arm and leg out to the side.

"Give me an *E!*"

"*E!*" I answered. Not knowing what part to use, I swung my arm and leg like a windmill in the other direction.

When I finally made it to the "And what does it spell?" part, even I didn't answer.

I dropped my arms, smiled my best cheerleader-type smile, raising my lower lip to cover my overbite, and felt the red blotches begin to form on my chest.

"Thank you," the teacher said, as she drew a line on her clipboard.

I felt like an absolute *idiot!* I wished the floor could have swallowed me up! I gave a quick nod to the cheerleading squad and finally moved my legs and walked out of the gym.

Sitting in the back of the late-afternoon bus, I tried to engrave the faces of the six cheerleaders in my mind. I felt really bad about hating them, but knew I'd spend the next three years avoiding them between classes. The bus dropped me off on top of Hilliard Avenue, and I found Mom outside on the Roanes' landing, hanging diapers out to dry. She pinned the corners two at a time and listened to my tale of woe.

". . . And if that wasn't bad enough, Mom," I explained, blinking back the moisture in my eyes, "I left my loafers in center court and had to go back and walk in front of *everyone* to get them!"

Mom clipped her last diaper to the line, gave me a wry smile, and said, "Well, Barbara Ann, next time you try out for cheerleading, you better know the cheers."

"Well, how obvious!" I snapped. "That's really, really helpful, Mom!" and with a quick look of indignation, I stomped into the house and ran up to the new girls' room on the third floor. The four girls had moved into the third floor of our house when Aunt Ethel and Uncle Herbie retired to Toms River and moved out.

I reached under my mattress to where I stashed my new box of filtered Parliaments, and lit a cigarette.

Meeting the King. Trump Tower. 1985.

I knew I wouldn't compromise my *Top 10 Condo Report* by changing any facts. But I also knew Mr. Trump would be outraged by his lowly ranking, and I didn't want my report to alienate an industry figure as powerful as Mr. Trump. So I had spent the weekend working the numbers every which way, and had figured out a way to do both. Once I found a solution, I practiced a routine on how to deliver it at least a dozen times. I stood in the elevator of Trump Tower with my heart racing, but my confidence intact.

The elevator doors opened into a reception area bigger than The Corcoran Group's entire office and backdropped with floor-to-ceiling views of Central Park. I stood in my new red suit atop all of New York.

A drop-dead gorgeous receptionist sat at the far end at a burled-wood desk. She was answering the phone. "Good morning, the Trump Organization," she said in a continuous loop. She was saying it with a lot more importance than I had ever been able to muster up for "Good morning, Giffuni Brothers." I made my way over to her desk and stood waiting to say hello. She looked to me like a beauty pageant queen, the kind you see on TV.

"Hi," I finally interrupted, offering my hand across her desk. "I'm Barbara Corcoran and I have an appointment with Mr. Trump."

She didn't look up, but lilted into an intercom, *"Bahr-bruh Cohr-krun* here to see Mr. Trump." Another beauty queen instantly appeared to escort me down a long wood-paneled hall. There yet another beauty queen asked that I follow her down another hall and passed me on to another woman who, unlike the others, looked like the kind of woman who could get some work done.

"Hello," she said with authority. "I'm Louise Sunshine. We spoke on the phone. If you'll wait here, I'll see if he's ready." She cracked a set of gigantic doors, stepped inside, and closed the doors behind her.

I thought about my new *Top 10 Condo Report*. As it was customary in New York to refer to apartments based on their sales price, my report ranked the top-ten-selling condos from the highest to the lowest sale price. I had pulled the figures from the *Yale Robbins Condo Report* and had also cross-checked each sale against the city's transfer files to make sure my numbers were absolutely correct.

A few moments later, the doors opened. "Mr. Trump will see you now," the woman announced, as she opened the doors and invited me into an office the size of an aircraft carrier.

Mr. Trump was seated behind a landing strip of a desk flanked by a panoramic view of Central Park. She gestured toward the two leather chairs positioned in front of his desk and announced, "Mr. Trump, this is Barbara Corcoran."

I walked over and extended my hand. When Mr. Trump took my hand, I filed it in my memory as the wimpiest handshake of all time. "I *really* appreciate your coming over," he cordially said, sizing me up and whisking his puffed blond helmet to the side. "Have a seat."

Before I reached the seat, he began, "I got your report and I don't agree with it. Your information is totally incorrect because there's sales data on Trump Tower you don't have access to."

As prepared as I thought I was, I was startled by his opening move. I felt my palms getting sticky. "Oh, really," I said politely, "and just what information is that, Mr. Trump?"

He leaned forward into the intercom that sat on the left corner of his desk and barked, "Norma! Bring me those condominium numbers!" The giant doors opened and a June Cleaver look-alike floated in, plunked a thick folder on Mr. Trump's otherwise clean desk, and floated out. He puckered his lips, opened the file, and leaned back in his chair. "If you'll take the time to look at these *recent* numbers," he emphasized, "it will be obvious to you that Trump Tower belongs at the top of your list!" He pushed the file in my direction, just out of reach.

I tried to move my chair closer to His Majesty's to get a peek at the numbers, but my chair wouldn't move. I stood up, took one giant step forward, opened the file, scanned the typed columns of sale prices, and recognized the information as the same data I had already used. *So far, so good,* I thought, knowing I had regained my footing.

"Mr. Trump," I said, "I'm pleased to say that each of these transactions was already *included* in my calculation." I smiled at him. "But I sure do appreciate your sharing them with me, sir."

Mr. Trump pursed his lips and bellowed into his intercom. "Marsha! Bring your calculator and come in here!" When the big doors parted again, an Ivana look-alike entered and strode across the floor in va-vooms to Mr. Trump's desk. Va-voom, va-voom, va-voom. She bent down, her cleavage eye level with Mr. Trump, and entered numbers as he rattled them off. When she came up with the same totals I already had, the ones that placed Trump Tower squarely in fourth place, Va-voom was dismissed.

Mr. Trump was clearly becoming more frustrated and barked once more at his intercom: "Joe! Get in here! Bring those Trump Tower deals we were just talking about this morning." Joe muscled in, a compact man in a too-tight suit. He reminded me of Rocky Rocciano, the drummer I dated from Garfield High. Joe handed a sheet of paper to Mr. Trump and muscled out. Mr. Trump nodded, passing the paper my way. "Have a look at *these* sales!" he said glibly.

I surveyed the sheet of twenty sale prices, each belonging to an apartment I hadn't seen before. The prices were much higher than the others, and Mr. Trump smirked when he saw the surprise register on my face. I shifted in my seat trying to get my routine back on track. "Could I see the dates on each of these transactions, Mr. Trump?" I asked.

To my relief, he bragged, "They were all sold this weekend, Barbara! All twenty of them! I tell you, it's incredible, really incredible!"

"That really *is* incredible, Mr. Trump!" I agreed. "And if they had *closed* this weekend, I could have included those sales in my report."

He winced, and I noticed his hair looked like cotton candy backlit by the western sky. "Listen," he said, enunciating each word, "*everyone knows that Trump Tower is the most expensive address in the world*, and putting anything else in your report is wrong."

The time had come for my grand finale, the moment to trump Trump.

"Mr. Trump," I began, "it's very important to me that I make you happy." I spoke slowly. "But I also need to publish a *truthful* report. Surely, there must be *something* you could think of that would make the report work for both of us."

And then, I made the move I had practiced a dozen times the night before. "Wait, wait just a minute!" I said, as if a lightbulb had just popped on in my head. I stood up, walked purposefully around to Mr. Trump's side of the desk, and leaned my forearm on his shoulder. "Let's see," I said, pointing to the Trump sale prices in my report. I paused a moment for dramatic effect. "What if we were to compute the prices on a *cost per foot basis*, instead of the total sale price like everyone else does? I wonder what that would do?"

I circled the highest-priced sale at Trump Tower, which was $3,033,500, divided it by its 2,509 square feet, and spit out the answer faster than a calculator. "Why that's one thousand two hundred nine dollars a square foot!" I concluded, drawing a circle around Apartment 62L and with an arrow moved it straight to the top of my "Top 10" list. I quickly divided Trump's next two most-expensive sales by their square footage, circled those answers, and moved them into second and third place.

"That's it! You've got it!" Trump enthused. "And I was just going to suggest it." The King of the Least for the Most was obviously pleased. "You know, Barbara, it puts Trump Tower exactly where it belongs—unmistakably the Most Expensive Address in the World!"

"And it's also honest," I said. I removed my arm from his shoulder, walked back around to the front of his desk, and offered my hand. "Thank you, Donald," I said. "You're a brilliant man and I really appreciate meeting you."

My new best friend stood up, shook my hand, and said, "You'll send me the revised copy, won't you?"

"I'd be happy to."

"Today?"

"Sure," I said. "I'll send it over by messenger this afternoon."

As the brass-paneled elevator door shut, I caught the image of me in my new red suit. I put my hands on my hips, looked straight into my eyes, and told my own reflection to:

"Give me a *Y! . . . Y!*" I said.

"Give me an *E! . . . E!*" I said.

"Give me an *S! . . . S!*" I said.

"What does it spell?"

"YES!" I cheered myself, thrusting my fist into the air.

I knew I had made the team.

Two days after the *Top 10 Condominium Report* was released to the press, Esther walked into my office holding up a copy of the *Wall Street Journal*. I could read the full-page ad from where I sat:

TRUMP TOWER

TOPS THE LIST

AS THE MOST

EXPENSIVE ADDRESS

IN THE WORLD! *

The asterisk referenced a bolded footnote at the bottom of the page. It had the words I most hoped to see, **"Source: *The Corcoran Report.*"**

The phone rang and I recognized Donald Trump's voice on the other end. "Hello, Barbara. Have you seen this morning's paper?"

"Yes, I have. I'm looking at it now."

"Well, how do you like it?" he asked with Trump-sized confidence.

"I like it a lot," I said, "but I wish you could have made our name a little bigger."

The following Monday, I opened the *New York Times* to yet another full-page ad.

ACCORDING TO

THE CORCORAN REPORT,

TRUMP TOWER

IS THE MOST EXPENSIVE

ADDRESS IN THE WORLD!

With equal billing in Trump's advertisement, The Corcoran Group became recognized as a major player in the New York real estate game.

✳

MOM'S LESSON #13: If you want to be a cheerleader, you better know the cheers.

✳

THE LESSON LEARNED
ABOUT BEING PREPARED

I've never met a smart person who wasn't overprepared, and after my cheerleading embarrassment, I swore I would never be unprepared again.

Donald Trump became my advocate simply because I was well prepared. If I hadn't put in the time, I couldn't have carried the meeting off with the confidence that I did.

1. **Preparation is the birthplace of confidence.**
   There's just no shortcut to a confident delivery. All good performances are a result of great preparation.

2. **Preparation takes time.**
   Showing up without having done the needed preparation is the equivalent of leaving on a long trip without packing a suitcase. Chances are you'll be cold when you get there.

3. **Self-doubt can be your very best friend.**
   Self-doubt always makes you overprepare. And when you overprepare, your success is guaranteed.

4. **There's no such thing as winging it.**
   Successful people might *appear* to be winging it, but they only look that way because they've practiced it a dozen times before.

5. **Whoever controls the agenda controls the meeting.**
   When *you* prepare the agenda, you're in control of 80 percent of the meeting, because everything you discuss will be in reaction to your ideas. A good agenda includes what your objective is and all the items you need to discuss in order to achieve it.

14

Go Stand Next to Nana and
See How Big You Are!

Fall 1985. Citibank Center.

"*With a sales staff of over fifty people and offices in Midtown and the Upper West Side . . .*"

The moderator's voice boomed through the auditorium in Citibank's corporate headquarters. I was being introduced to an audience of 800 people, about 750 more people than I'd ever addressed.

"*. . . Ms. Corcoran also publishes* The Corcoran Report, *today considered the bible of the New York real estate market . . .*"

Citibank's invitation to speak at the company's first "Seminar for Home Buyers" had caught me by surprise. When the man from the bank's events department called, he enthusiastically explained that my recent comments on home buying in the *Wall Street Journal* made me an ideal speaker for their new seminar. And, he promised, the featured speakers would be well promoted weeks before the event. I figured that kind of free advertising would be great for my business.

"I have no doubt Ms. Corcoran's tips on home buying will help you . . ."

It was my first public speech and I had worked on it for three weeks, editing every word and rehearsing its delivery over and over again in my mind. With the *Quick and Easy Way to Effective Speaking* as my guide, I had typed the first line of each of my paragraphs in caps on separate index cards. I was ready!

". . . So please join me in welcoming the president of The Corcoran Group, Barbara Corcoran!"

The audience broke into applause. I stood up, raised my chin to create just the right look of confidence, and made my way behind the two other chairs to center stage. *You are a PRO-fessional speaker!* a happy little voice in my head whispered, *you're a Natural, a real natural!* I stepped behind the podium and gracefully placed my left hand on the edge. I took one serious look down at my notes, looked up at the audience, flashed my best smile, and with a quick wave of my right hand chirped, "Hello, there!"

I had decided to open Cosby-style with a well-rehearsed joke. "Did you hear the one about the banker who was a *great lover?*" I began. I leaned into the podium, just as planned, and waited for the audience's reply. Sixteen hundred eyes stared back at me, but not one offered a response. The little voice inside my head encouraged, *Go on, go on, you're doing fine!* But something in my heart made me wonder.

When I realized that the audience was waiting for the punch line, I decided I'd better give them the answer. *Oh, my God*, my mind shrieked. *What is the punch line?* I quickly looked down at index card #1. It read, "DID YOU HEAR THE ONE ABOUT THE BANKER WHO'S A GREAT LOVER?" That's all. I shuffled the card to the back of my deck and sneaked a peek at card #2. And it read, "WHAT'S YOUR BUDGET?" That's all.

I began to panic and the little voice inside my head began to scream. *Why didn't you write the answer, stupid! Just think! Say something! Say ANYTHING!* No matter how hard I tried, I just couldn't remember the punch line. I smoothed down the front of my new red suit, took a big breath, and decided to move on.

When I looked back down at my "WHAT'S YOUR BUDGET?" card, the words had turned blurry. But I knew the rest of this point anyway and started to speak, but nothing came out. I tried to cough and couldn't. I tried again to speak, make a sound, any sound, but I couldn't. I realized that my voice wasn't going to come out, not tonight, not any night, not ever again.

I glanced over to the moderator, and he looked as scared as I felt. So I turned to the audience and opened my mouth as wide as I could. Pointing to the mute hole, I slowly shook my head no. I turned and took what seemed to be a very long walk back to my seat.

The moderator jumped up and rushed to the microphone. "Okay . . ." he said, looking bewildered. "Thank you, Barbara! And we'll be hearing more from her later. Next, I'd like to introduce Citibank's leading mortgage specialist . . ."

I spent the rest of the seminar sitting in my chair and numbly staring at the Citibank logo.

I was still burning from public humiliation as I got home and sank into a hot bath. The night's calamity played again and again in my mind; with each rerun I grew smaller and smaller.

Winter. The kitchen table.

We had been sent home that Friday afternoon with our midyear report cards with the Sisters' usual instructions to bring them back Monday morning along with our parent's signature. We all anxiously waited at the kitchen table as Dad looked over and signed our cards one by one.

"That's excellent work, Ellen." He beamed, looking down her column of A's and signing "Rock Hudson" at the bottom. Everyone laughed and Ellen leaned over his shoulder to have a better look. "And you did a nice job there, Tommy, but let's turn that B in gym into an A next time." Tommy danced off through the living room with Elliott Ness's signature. Awaiting Mr. Corcoran's signatures had become a quarterly event for the St. Joseph's Sisters at the Holy Rosary School. They always looked forward to the Mondays we brought our signed report cards back.

"Eddie," Dad continued, shifting his voice into low gear, "four F's are two too many! Another three months' garbage duty for you! Now for you, Barbara Ann," Dad said, as he took my report card in his hand and I took a quiet step back toward the refrigerator, "well, at least you're consistent. Straight D's from top to bottom!" All the kids laughed as Dad handed me the report card signed by Pat Boone.

I ran to my room, jumped on my bed, and buried my face in the pillow, feeling ashamed to be so stupid.

"Barbara," Mom said as she sat on the edge of my bed, "don't be so hard on yourself, straight D's aren't that bad. And, besides, Sister Joseph Marie always tells me you're the nicest girl in the whole class." I turned my head to look at my mother. "Now," she said, "get yourself up and go stand next to Nana and see how big you are."

Nana was almost four feet eight inches tall, but picked up another two inches as she trotted around the house in her everyday pumps. She was standing next to the sofa and folding towels on the coffee table. Nana's big white pocketbook, the constant companion that scraped the ground as she walked, was looped around her left arm.

"Hi, Nana," I said, "Mom sent me to see how big I am." Nana smiled as she took off her shoes and turned her back against mine.

"Oh, look!" she exclaimed over her shoulder, "you're even bigger than last time!" I gave Nana a hug, she put on her shoes, and I ran out the screen door to go play with my friends.

* * *

The morning after my Citibank debacle, I picked up the New York University Continuing Education circular from my desk and called the phone number listed on the back. "I'd like to teach a course," I told the nice woman at the school.

"Oh, on what subject?" she asked sweetly.

"A course on what every real estate salesperson should know," I said, quickly adding, "And I'm more than qualified to teach. I've hired and trained more than fifty salespeople, I have great material, and I'm also an *excellent* speaker!"

"Well, then, why don't you submit a course outline, and send it to the program office care of Mr. Neil Boffey," she suggested. "If he likes it, he'll pass it along to the program committee, who may approve it for the summer program."

I smiled and put down the phone.

June 1986. New York University.

My seven students appeared to be a contingent sent over from the United Nations. Just like the rest of New York, they were a smorgasbord of different nationalities and they were all serious about being there. Since most of the seats were empty, I decided there must have been a mix-up in the room number given to the students, and delayed starting the class. I hoped that another dozen or so students would be arriving late to fill the desks.

"We'll begin class in about five minutes," I announced, "to give the other students a chance to arrive. But while we wait, why don't we go around the room and introduce ourselves to one another? Please speak up, give us your name first, and then, if you'd like, tell me what you hope to get out of the class over the next ten weeks." I listened and smiled as the students introduced themselves.

"Let me also introduce myself to you. I'm Barbara Corcoran, president of The Corcoran Group." I took a quick look down at my notes and said, "Since it looks tonight as though we're only going to be seven, let's begin."

No sooner had I said "seven," than the door banged open and a Chinese woman hurried in. She walked directly to the center front desk and said to the man sitting there, "I want to sit there." The man looked confused and started to move.

"There's another seat in the front over here," I quickly interrupted. "And it also has a better view of the blackboard. As everyone just finished introducing themselves, why don't you take a seat and introduce yourself to the class."

"Carrie Chiang," she blurted, and then hustled over to the desk on the other side of the room and plopped herself down. While I went over the classroom rules, she ruffled through her papers and unpacked her bags.

"I was asked to announce that smoking and eating in the classroom are not permitted, but as six-thirty is my dinner hour, you're welcome to bring food, as long as you leave the room as clean as you found it." The woman hiding her sandwich looked relieved. "You'll find the rest rooms down the hall and we'll be taking a break in about an hour. Last, I'm pleased to announce that everyone will earn an A for taking this course simply because you came. Your outline is in front of you, so let's get started." The students seemed to like my A idea and smiled.

The best way to get over my Citibank debacle was to move on, and I knew I could only do that by practicing speaking in front of a large group. Although lecturing to eight students wasn't exactly what I had in mind, I looked at the class and figured some practice was better than no practice at all.

An hour later, I declared a class break and walked down the hall to the school cafeteria. I had made up my mind to cancel the remaining nine classes and would announce it right after the break. Giving up three hours every Monday night for ten weeks over the summer just wasn't going to be worth it.

As I reached for the wilted fruit salad, I was startled to hear my name. "Baa-bwa!" the Chinese woman called as she cut into the line and made her way toward me. "Baa-bwa, you know how long I been in business? You know how long?"

"No, I don't," I answered, picking up a bagel and cream cheese from the counter. "How long has it been?"

"T'ree months," she bragged.

"Three months?" I repeated.

"You know how much money I make in t'ree months?"

"No, I don't," I said, surprised that someone would offer so much information so quickly, especially in a crowded cafeteria line.

"*Two, hundred, dousand, dollars!*" she bragged, loud enough for the buzz in the line to come to a complete stop. "I sell only condos," she said. "I sell lots of condos!"

"Selling condos?" I said aloud. "How can you make that much money selling only condos?!" I took a closer look at her, trying to pick up anything about her that lacked credibility. But everything about her looked like the genuine article: her blunt-cut, neatly combed hair, her solid gold choker, her well-tailored sweater set with three buttons open and three buttons closed. Even her black mid-height heels, supporting two sturdy legs, looked as if they meant business. Miss Chiang started speaking in a rapid-fire, Chinese-American dialect, gesturing frantically as she spoke.

"I sell *big* condos to big customer in Hong Kong!" she rattled, opening up her leather file cabinet and pulling out a manila folder. "He's a *big* customer, he send me his cousin and his cousin buy small condo. Dis lady have sister-in-law in Taiwan and she buy *two* condos! She send me sister's *cousin* in Hong Kong, but she no good. But she send me cousin from Taiwan and she buy *more* condo!"

I immediately switched gears from snoozing to schmoozing, realizing I had just stepped in front of the Hong Kong to Taiwan to New York Express. "That's *really* incredible!" I admired. "You're *just* amazing!" I gave Miss Chiang my very best smile and decided the ten weeks might be worth it after all!

✳

MOM'S LESSON #14: Go stand next to Nana and see how big you are!

✳

THE LESSON LEARNED ABOUT STANDING TALL

On bad days, my mother used Nana to reframe our perspective and make us feel better. She never once suggested that we measure ourselves against anyone tall. And just as my mother changed our perspective then, I was able to reframe the Citibank debacle that night. I realized that at least I got up there, and did have something to say. I just couldn't say it then.

My Citibank flop only made me try harder, and by getting back up, I was able to recruit the best condominium salesperson in all New York. By the time the NYU semester ended, Carrie Chiang had arrived at our office along with her leather file cabinet, her twelve boxes of folders, and her first cousin working as her assistant.

When Carrie started in 1986, the condominium market accounted for less than 5 percent of the city's residential sales. By late 2002, New York's burgeoning condo market accounted for more than 35 percent of city sales. And Carrie Chiang, New York's number 1 undisputed Condo Queen, had sold more condos than anyone else.

By teaching the classes at NYU over the next five years, I succeeded in becoming an excellent public speaker, and the course proved to be my most fertile ground for recruiting top-notch salespeople. Not a bad payoff for standing back up.

What I've learned about public failures is that *nobody really gives a damn!* While you're wallowing around worrying about what people are thinking, you fail to notice that everybody else has already moved on. And fretting about what the other guy thinks often stops you from trying in the first place.

15

If You Want to Get Noticed,
Write Your Name on the Wall

Summer. Mrs. Cacciotti's.

"**B**arbara Ann," my mother said sharply with her hands on the waist of her blue housedress, "did *you* write your name on Mrs. Cacciotti's wall?"

"Why?" I answered, trying to buy a little time.

"Don't you why me, Barbara!" Mom commanded. "*Did* you?"

"I *think* so," I said with hesitation.

"Well, then, Barbara, if you *think* so, you better start *thinking* about coming with me!" Mom grabbed my wrist and yanked me out the screen door. From how fast we were walking, I was starting to get the feeling I might be in trouble.

Mrs. Cacciotti's house was four doors down, and with each step toward it, I was growing more fearful. Mrs. Cacciotti had called only minutes ago, so I knew Mom hadn't actually *seen* what I'd done.

* * *

For two whole weeks, Janet Cleary, Eugene Darby, and I met on the strip of grass across the street from Mrs. Cacciotti's house and watched the three men build a long retaining wall in front of her house. As they laid the cement blocks one by one, they didn't talk much, but from the few words they said, we knew they weren't from Edgewater.

On the last day they were there, the men took what looked like a pointy spatula and smoothed cement all over the front of the wall just like Mom iced her cake. It wasn't until Eugene and Janet went home for dinner that I saw my opportunity.

I made a beeline to Mrs. Cacciotti's wall to figure out how long it was. I began where the wall started and took broad steps around the curve to where it joined Mrs. Mertz's driveway. The whole wall was a total of fifteen big steps. *Perfect!* I thought. *Just exactly what I need.*

I picked up a big stick from Mrs. Mertz's yard and walked back to where the wall started and drew the top of the first *B* about level with my bangs. I made the two sideway bumps nice and round, ending the bottom bump with a fancy curlicue. I took two side steps to the right and drew an *A*. (I had to go back and add a little extra line on the right side to make the legs even.) When I finished the *N* on the far side facing Mrs. Mertz's, I wiped off my stick on her grass and stepped back to take a good look at my work of art.

"BARBARA CORCORAN?!" my mother cried as we came upon my masterpiece. "Barbara Ann, what were you thinking?!"

What I was thinking was: *Why couldn't I have just written "Barbara"?* There were a few Barbaras in Edgewater, but only *one* "Barbara Corcoran." And that was the one written on Mrs. Cacciotti's wall.

"How could you do that?" my mother scowled, leaning into my face. "And where was your brain? Don't you know if you write your name on a wall, somebody's going to notice?"

I knew it wasn't the kind of question Mom really wanted an

answer to. But I was thinking that I sort of knew somebody would notice, and, in fact, that was the whole idea. I just didn't know *Mom* was going to notice!

I was sentenced to two weeks of hard labor as Mrs. Cacciotti's slave. Mom instructed me to knock on her door every morning at eight and say, "Good morning, Mrs. Cacciotti! What can I do for you today?"

I always got the feeling that Mrs. Cacciotti had to think hard to come up with stuff for me to do. But for two weeks I put Mrs. Cacciotti's milk bottles outside for Mr. Colontoni, the milkman, walked her brown dog, and swept her front steps. I cleaned up the clippings from her hedges and pulled some weeds from her backyard. I didn't like working for Mrs. Cacciotti much, but I was still happy I wrote on her wall.

My name was famous on Undercliff Avenue for two whole days! On the third day, the same three men came back, and Mom paid them to erase my name from Mrs. Cacciotti's wall.

✳

MOM'S LESSON #15: If you want to get noticed, write your name on the wall.

✳

THE LESSON LEARNED
ABOUT GETTING NOTICED

By growing up in a family of ten kids, I learned how to grab attention in a crowded market. I would later learn how to steal the limelight in a city of eight million. Getting publicity is nothing more than getting attention.

All reporters have one problem. They need stories. And when you provide reporters with a good story idea, you're *not* asking for a favor, you're giving them a gift.

The Corcoran Group typically spends $5 million a year on advertising, but less than $100,000 on publicity. Advertising helped us make our name, but publicity put it on the marquee.

Unlike advertising, publicity has the power of the third-party endorsement, which builds credibility around a name. If a company spends millions of dollars advertising how good they are, some people may believe it. But if a major newspaper presents the company in a favorable light, *everyone* believes it.

Publishing our statistics in *The Corcoran Report* was the beginning of what would later prove to be my most profitable road to success. Statistics are the slam dunk of all publicity. But there are other ways to capture media attention. Here's how:

1. **Making news on hearsay or rumors.**

   Sometimes the easiest story to get publicity on is the one that's already out there. It's like tying your wagon onto someone else's horse.

2. **Making news with your competitor's sales.**

   The irony of most businesses is that you often can't talk about your own sales, either for privacy or legal reasons. But you can *always* talk about your competitor's sales, and in doing so, you will inevitably get the credit.

3. **Good old-fashioned grandstanding.**

   Everyone loves a show. Grandstanding is nothing more than trying to figure out what would be visually interesting and be a little different from the norm.

Here are a few ways we've made headlines:

THE LITTLE PINK BUILDING ON EAST 52nd STREET

When we were confronted with marketing our first new building project, it was already labeled a pink elephant that couldn't be sold. I took its liability and made it an asset by painting the building pink. By naming it the "Pink Elephant," we rode the publicity for all it was worth, and the affection it generated sold out the building in three months' time.

MADONNA GOES HOUSEHUNTING

When I read in the paper that Madonna was on the hunt for a new apartment, I was disappointed to learn that none of our salespeople were working with her. I immediately made a checklist of what Madonna would be looking for. All I knew was that she lived in a large apartment on the West Side and that she was about to have a baby. The checklist included the usual things important to any wealthy celebrity, such as grand space, top security, views, and all the luxury amenities that money can buy. I sent out a copy of the list to all our media contacts that same day. Everyone received a copy, except Madonna.

Two hours later, I was sitting at a desk at CNN's Penn Plaza studio, chatting it up on-air. I was no more an authority on what Madonna's wish list might include than anybody else, but I was the only one willing to speculate.

Everyone in our marketplace wrongly assumed that Madonna was *our* client, and we got four other celebrities as a result of the publicity.

AMERICAN INDIAN RITUAL SELLS HOME

After six months of trying to sell an eleven-room Park Avenue apartment, our efforts proved unsuccessful. We were baffled as to why until we uncovered the awful truth that the apartment had been the stage for a prolonged and violent marriage. In an attempt to satisfy the disgruntled seller when he threatened to pull the listing, we recommended "a complete smudging of the apartment."

Smudging is an American Indian ritual performed with bells and incense to cleanse troublesome spaces of their evil spirits. The ancient blessing had to be followed by twenty-four hours of total darkness with the shades drawn and all light eliminated. The next morning, we opened the curtains and the first couple to see it sat on the bed in the master bedroom and eagerly offered the full $3.2 million asking price.

After this success, we made a regular practice of offering our smudging services for problem apartments. We never again performed them without a newspaper reporter or television crew present.

HELPING ROVER PASS THE CO-OP BOARD

As "no dog" buildings became commonplace, and as rules surrounding pet behavior became more ridiculous, we hired a celebrity dog trainer to teach our clients' dogs how to pass co-op boards. Although the boards had not actually *asked* any dogs to come in for a board interview, we made our dogs ready nonetheless!

The publicity our stunt generated gave me a sore back from bending over to shake doggie paws, as newspaper photographers snapped away!

THE $35 MILLION FIXER UPPER

When Sharon Baum, New York City's grand dame of multimillion-dollar home sales, asked me to survey the Vanderbilt Mansion on East Sixty-fourth Street, we found twenty-two rooms eerily frozen in time. The original gas lanterns were still in place, along with the old iceboxes in the basement kitchen. Sharon set the price at $35 million and estimated it needed another $10 million to make it livable.

I billed the mansion as "The $35 Million Fixer-Upper" and the curiosity about the property not only brought eleven camera crews, but also more than three dozen multimillionaires asking to see the property.

KENNEDY LOFT PUT ON BLOCK

A *New York Post* reporter called only minutes after John F. Kennedy, Jr., and his glamorous young wife, Carolyn Bessette, were declared dead in a tragic plane crash. The reporter urgently asked what Kennedy's Tribeca loft would be worth if it was put on the market for sale. Still surprised by the call, I calculated out loud that six months earlier we had sold an identical apartment one floor below the JFK, Jr. loft for a million dollars. The market had been active, so I figured its value had increased by about a half million since. I added another million for the Kennedy loft's "celebrity value" and declared, "I guess the value would be somewhere around $2.5 million."

I was shocked to read the next morning's *New York Post* headline: "KENNEDY LOFT PUT ON BLOCK FOR $2.5 MILLION" with me quoted as the authority. My phone rang all day, the story was carried on every major network, and I became the spokeswoman for the John Jr. loft even though it was not even for sale.

Three months later, my competitor got the listing and listed it at $2.5 million, but they were required to sign a nondisclosure agreement. So, who do you think the press called?

The property finally sold to actor Ed Burns for . . . $2.5 million. We never listed it and we never sold it, but when Dan Rather's *Evening News*, *CNN*, and *Entertainment Tonight* covered the record-breaking sale, I was again featured as the expert "Broker to the Stars."

NEW YORK'S HIGHEST PRICED SALE

When a Park Avenue triplex sold for the record-breaking price of $37 million, our competitor who sold it was sworn to secrecy. When the competitor refused to speak to the press, the press soon called me. I quickly labeled the sale a "steal of a deal" and by that evening, I was on CBS News and the anchor was introducing me as the woman who made the highest-priced sale in history. I graciously corrected him, but still everyone in New York continued to think we had made the highest-priced sale in history.

WHAT TO DO WHEN
THE REPORTER CALLS

1. Drop everything.

When my husband wants to reach me, he says he's calling from the *New York Times*. I've learned that the first person the reporter reaches *makes* the story, and the next person only *confirms* the story. The person who makes the story always gets the quotes. When the reporter calls, pick up the phone.

2. Deliver what you promise and deliver it fast.

With the advent of e-mail, information is immediately available. I use e-mail to reach my salespeople and ferret out whatever minutiae a reporter may need for his story. I think of our public relations staff members as a service department immediately available to any newspaper, magazine, or television station that might call.

3. Talk short. Talk plain.

You might *feel* more astute explaining to a reporter that "marketplace conditions have declined somewhat and I have every confidence that economic conditions will improve blah, blah,

blah." But if your competitor says, "The market dumped," that's the quote you'll see in the morning paper.

4. **Always tell the truth.** *Always.*

It's in the worst of times that publicity is your very best friend. When the stock market tanked in 1987, New York City real estate prices dropped by 40 percent, as did our commissions. But as my competitors ran for cover, I took center stage. I used the media to build my business, knowing that bad news is good news in the media world.

TIPS ON PUTTING YOUR BEST FACE FORWARD

1. **If you want to be noticed, dress the part.**

My red suit became my trademark. Everyone noticed me when I had it on.

2. **Schedule your photo shoots the day you arrive back from vacation.**

You'll take your best picture when you're fully rested. Hire a professional makeup artist to help you look your best.

3. **Paint your office wall in your best color.**

Decide what color you look best in and paint your wall that shade and prominently display your company name on it. Since most camera crews prefer to interview executives at their desks, you'll be backed by your best color and your logo will be in the shot.

16

Sweep the Corners and the
Whole House Stays Clean

Summer 1987. The Corcoran Group.

"Okay, ladies," I said, pointing to the list of names on the conference room table and taking in a slow, deep breath. "I know you don't want to fire these people, and I genuinely like each one as much as you do. But the fact remains you've done everything you possibly could for them, and, frankly, these fourteen salespeople will never succeed in the business."

My companions at the conference room table, Esther and our West Side manager, Barbara Brine, gave me a blank look. Like our last two meetings on the same subject, our discussion was going nowhere. Esther had reluctantly prepared a list ranking our fifty-two salespeople in order of production and was as shocked as I was to see that the top 10 percent of our salespeople were making 80 percent of the company's money. Meanwhile, the bottom 25 percent of our salespeople were draining resources without adding anything back.

Our cost of doing business had climbed along with apartment

prices, and our overhead per agent was running $40,000 a year. With the real estate market at a healthy boil, when one agent didn't produce, the next agent's production was big enough to pick up the slack. But I was worried about what would happen if the market braked and slowed to a simmer. Even someone who failed algebra twice could do the math.

My sales managers had already met with each of their salespeople in the bottom of the list, only to come back and give me a long dissertation on how those who were failing were "really trying their best."

I was stumped and identified with the managers' enormous discomfort. I was asking them to do what I couldn't do myself, and it rendered my order impotent. I found that firing anyone, even when it's the right thing to do, always felt wrong. So lacking the courage to say, *"Just fire them,"* I could only muster, "So, when will you ask them to leave?"

Esther stiffened in her chair, and Barbara Brine looked at the list and sighed. "Four of the bottom ten have never made a deal," Barbara admitted, "but the other six have made almost twenty thousand dollars each and that's certainly better than having an empty desk!"

"No, that's not how it works," I insisted. "With an overhead of forty thousand, that's twenty thousand dollars *short* for each desk! If you multiply *that* times six desks, that's a *hundred-and-twenty-thousand-dollar loss*! We might be in a fat market now, and getting away with it, but if the market goes south, we'll be dead on arrival."

What I really wanted to say was: *Listen! I've been talking to you about cleaning up this mess for three months now and nothing has changed! What do I have to do to move this thing along? I won't carry the deadwood any longer. We've got to clean up our mess and we've got to do it now!*

But what I said instead was: "How about we go to the movies?" It seemed the more attainable option.

Esther and Barbara looked bewildered, and then relieved. Barbara spoke first: "That sounds like a lovely idea. Doesn't it, Esther?"

We left the office and spent the rest of the afternoon drooling over Mel Gibson in *Lethal Weapon*.

Fall. Hilliard Avenue.

We were halfway up Hilliard Avenue when my older sister Denise and I saw our house through the school bus window. There were lots of colored streamers dangling in the big side-yard tree, and the front retaining wall was draped with dozens of brightly colored flags.

"Whose birthday is it?" Denise asked.

"Don't know," I said, turning and squinting my eyes to get a better look. "Maybe it's Tommy's?"

"Nah, his was last month, but it could be Eddie's. Isn't his after Tommy's?"

"Well, *whosever* birthday it is, it sure looks like Mom outdid herself this time!"

As we neared our house at the top of the hill, the wall decorations began to look less like a party and more like a mess. "De-Denise!" I stammered, nudging her arm and pointing. "Isn't that your new green sweater on the front wall?"

"What!?" she gasped, covering her mouth with both hands.

"Oh, God!" I said, slumping down into the bus seat. "Don't look now, but I think our bras are hanging in the tree!"

By now every kid on the bus had rushed the left windows, pushing each other aside for a better look. Denise slid down eye level with me and whispered, "*It's our clothes, I think maybe all of them, and they're all over the yard!*"

"Getting off!?" the bus driver shouted back through the catcalls. I grabbed Denise's arm and we made our escape through the accordion doors. "Don't look," I directed through clenched teeth, "just keep walking straight ahead and pretend we live at the Clearys' house."

"*Nice panties!*" a boy shouted as the bus pulled away. We walked on, our faces flushed. Denise was swearing under her breath.

"*Who?*" my sister hissed. "*Who* would have done such a *disgusting thing?*"

Together we answered, "*Mom!*"

Mom liked a clean house and surprised us on more than one occasion when she appeared in the girls' room, broom and dustpan in hand, eager to demonstrate her theory on housecleaning.

Mom believed in sweeping corners. First she pulled all the furniture away from the walls, and jammed her broom into the nearest corner. Next, she followed the woodwork around clockwise, sweeping the dirt toward the center of the room as she went. Then she pushed the furniture back against the walls, scooped up the dirt pile with her dustpan, and dumped it into a brown paper bag. "Now, remember, girls," she said as she finished a cleaning demonstration. "If you sweep the corners, the whole house stays clean."

When the girls moved upstairs into the new girls' room, Mom made Saturday cleaning *our* responsibility, but we took our extra freedom and ran with it. After we failed Mom's weekly inspections a few times, she began to threaten us with: "If you don't take care of your room in a proper fashion, *I'm* going to take care of it for you!"

Mom had made good on her promise.

Denise and I ran up the two flights to our room, and surveyed it in horror. Our beds had been stripped. Our blankets were gone, our pillows were gone, and every drawer in our dresser was open and empty. Our room looked as if we had moved out. Only the pink-checked curtains remained, flapping back and forth in the open window.

I walked over and sat down on my bare mattress and reached under it. I was relieved to find my pack of cigarettes undiscovered. "Want a smoke?" I asked Denise as I pulled one out. It was only a filter. I pulled out another, and it was a filter. I dumped out the whole box. Mom had cut every cigarette into thirds and put them, filters up, back in the box. I threw the box across the room into the empty trash can, and lay back on my bed.

"Look!" Denise shrieked. I followed her pointing arm. Six-inch letters, scrawled across our dresser mirror in Mom's signature white shoe polish, denounced us as:

PIGS!

"Size eight," I told the woman behind the counter at Celine's Boutique on Park Avenue. We were walking back from *Lethal Weapon* when I spotted the pink suede shoes in the window. The shoes must have been for the woman who had everything. They had little pink bunny ears attached to the front, a set of rolling glass eyes beneath curly black lashes, and a black sculpted nose attached to a set of long bunny whiskers.

"That will be two hundred and twenty-two dollars, please," the woman behind the counter said. Esther and Barbara Brine looked at me as if I had lost my mind as I wrote out the check.

When I got back to the office, I removed my new bunny shoes from their box and placed them on my desk. I took out the list of nonproductive salespeople and reached for a cube of paper.

"H. H.," I wrote on the first small yellow square.

"A. Z.," I wrote on the next.

"S. K.," I wrote on the one after that and continued until all ten of the salespeople's initials were written on individual squares. I folded the papers in half, then in quarters, and then in eighths. I dropped five of the tiny notes in each shoe, placed the bunnies back in their box, and taped my handwritten note to Barbara Brine on top. It read:

BB:
Ask these people
to hop on out
of here by <u>Friday</u>!
    —Barb
      xx

I sealed the box and sent it by messenger to the West Side office.

Within an hour of getting the shoes, Barbara Brine called. She was laughing, and said she'd "hop right to it."

✳

MOM'S LESSON #16: Sweep the corners and the whole house stays clean.

✳

THE LESSON LEARNED ABOUT KEEPING THE HOUSE CLEAN

The bunny shoes allowed me to dress something disagreeable as more agreeable. I succeeded in making the dreadful topic of firing a bit friendlier and gave myself the courage to set the needed deadline.

The $222 bunny shoes saved The Corcoran Group $120,000 that year. The money was no longer being spent to support the bottom 25 percent of nonproductive salespeople. Using the 25 percent rule, we've been cleaning out the corners of our company ever since.

Firing people is the least popular task of any manager, and those who are the best at hiring are usually the worst at firing. My managers were great recruiters and loved their salespeople. But they were leading with their hearts instead of their heads.

Firing is also a personal admission that you hired the wrong person, that your judgment was wrong. But even with the most arduous screening and choosing, in real estate sales only one in six salespeople make it. In fact, in most real estate brokerage companies, more than half the salespeople don't meet their desk costs even after two years in the business. Nothing is more deceiving than a desk that looks productive simply because someone is sitting there.

Here are the four ways I sweep the corners and keep my sales house clean:

1. Fire Before You Hire.

Create a method to keep track of each new salesperson's progress so you can fire the nonproductive ones before they get lost in the shuffle.

DAY 1. During the interview, state your expectations clearly.

Tell the would-be salesperson that they have a limited time to produce their first sale. In the real estate sales business, that translates into one signed contract within the first ninety days.

DAY 30. Schedule a meeting with each new salesperson.

The purpose is to check their progress and offer them the help they might need.

DAY 60. Extend or keep the deadline.

By Day 60, salespeople begin to panic. As great salespeople are sometimes slow starters, it's the manager's option to either stick to the ninety-day deadline or take off the pressure with a stay of execution. If you're confident that the salesperson is on the right track, now's the time to extend a benevolent hand to help him across the finish line.

D-DAY. By ninety days, the nonproducers fire themselves.
Because the expectations were stated clearly on Day 1, nonproducers can plan for their own departure and leave with dignity before the deadline. And a well-defined exit strategy allows the manager to feel fair as the salesperson says good-bye.

2. **Know the Cost of Each Desk.**
    The starting gate of making any sales organization productive is to know how much each salesperson must produce to turn a profit. Simply divide your total yearly overhead (including expected expansion costs and profits) and divide the figure by the number of salespeople in your organization. With your eyes wide open, you'll work toward making every desk productive.

3. **Clean Out the Bottom 25 Percent.**
    The 25 percent rule is simply this: When a salesperson remains in the bottom 25 percent of the company for more than one quarter, the individual is reviewed for possible notice of termination.

    Here are the three steps that make this system work:

    1. Make a list of your salespeople in order of production.
    Do it every quarter. The idea here is to purge the company of its deadwood, that is, the bottom 25 percent of the salesforce.

    2. Fire a warning shot.
    Meet with each underachiever and find out what you could do to help them turn their production around. Put the plan on paper.

3. *Establish a deadline.*

The deadline should be reasonable and match your degree of confidence in the individual's ability to become productive. A clearly stated deadline is a surefire way of finding out who can swim. Usually only one in four does.

4. Allow One Pet per Office.

Our sales managers can choose to keep one nonproductive salesperson. This is usually an individual who the manager believes helps the whole group in some collective way—someone, for example, who boosts office morale or helps the team. It's the sales manager's equivalent of a "governor's pardon," and we affectionately call the policy "One pet per office."

Firing is never easy. By establishing clear parameters, we built a reliable system for making our company highly productive. It was also a lot more efficient than having the bunny shoes hop all over town.

Here are some tips to keeping firing friendly:

1. Fire with someone else present.

When you sit down to break the bad news, it's sometimes easier to do it with another manager present. That person not only provides moral support, but you hold each other accountable for getting the job done.

2. Ask for their permission to be honest with them.

Ask, "Do you mind if I'm honest with you?" Everyone always agrees, and everyone really prefers honesty.

3. Tell them the truth.

Nothing is worse than being hanged when you don't know what the crime is. It's simply not fair, and it leaves the person wondering for the rest of his life.

4. Always start by telling them what they do well.

When you fire someone, you want to ensure that they leave with their self-esteem intact. If you take the time to prepare a list of what they do well and acknowledge it, it will be easier for them to accept your critique of why they're not suited for their present job.

5. Cut to the chase.

Someone being fired doesn't want to spend a lot of time discussing it. Tell them what you tell them and make your good-bye short.

17

In a Family, Everyone Helps
Mash the Potatoes

Spring 1989. New York City.

We had just signed a new lease for five thousand fancy feet of space on Madison Avenue when the stock market crashed in October '87. Black Monday sent the economy into a tailspin and real estate into a freefall.

Things only got worse. By the spring of 1989, after a year and a half of juggling our finances and begging our creditors for more time, our bills were piling up faster than our commissions. Putting deals together had become an impossible task. I had to agree with Esther when she said she wished we had some cash reserves.

Esther had our bills laid out in stacks on the conference room table. Her neatly written note on top read, "Barb, you better have a look."

I sat down and riffled through the piles. The biggest stack was from the advertising agency. It stood eight inches high and totaled more than $100,000. I was happy to note that per my instruction, both the office rent and the payroll were paid to date, but according to my quick calculation, we owed another $200,000 for printing, office supplies, equipment leases, insurance, accounting fees, and telephone. I added up our accounts receivable, and if our deals closed within the next four months as projected, our net commissions would total only $36,000.

"Whew," I gasped, shaking the number out of my head, "that leaves us with a shortfall of two hundred sixty-four thousand dollars!" I pulled the tape from the adding machine, circled the red figure, walked to my desk, and hid it in my file drawer.

When I reached for my purse, I found a note clipped to it. It read, "Don't forget we have the $300,000 credit line at Citibank." (Signed) "Esther."

Dad's La-Z-Boy. Edgewater.

Mom was in her usual rush down the rickety wooden stairs, which led from the bathroom to the cellar, when she took a bad fall and broke her ankle in two places. She was on her way to check the furnace, which kicked off whenever the Roanes filled their tub at the same time we did. She was trying to get down and back before the breaded veal patties burned in the frying pan.

Even with her leg in a cast, Mom kept charging at full throttle. She hopped up and down the front steps on her good leg, almost as fast as we ran them on two. She had a wheelchair, a walker, crutches, and, most important, another foot.

Mom altered her daily routines to accommodate the new annoyance and used her walker as a temporary clothesline, draping things over it as if it were a drying rack. She discovered that by wrapping the heel of her crutch with a damp rag and a rubber band, she could reach into the tight spots to clean out the cobwebs. Her wheelchair soon sat parked in the side yard, where it served as a temporary stool for peeling potatoes.

Mom's new condition didn't change Dad's routine at all. Each night before leaving for his second job as night watchman at the Lever Brothers Co., Dad still settled into his La-Z-Boy chair in the living room for his evening smoke. He opened his tin of Half and Half Tobacco, took a large pinch, and carefully stuffed his burled-wood pipe. After a few puffs, he leaned back, rested his pipe on a beanbag ashtray, cocked his head back and fell asleep. That was Dad's routine, and that's where he sat the night Mom lost it.

It was shortly before dinner and Mom was crutching around the kitchen, hopping back and forth between the sink, refrigerator, and stove. Baby Jeanine was on her hip and Marty Joe was pulling at her hem. Ellen and I were setting the table.

Mom finished draining the potatoes and dumped them and a stick of butter into her big aluminum pot. She hopped over to the refrigerator, took out the milk, and poured some into the potatoes. With her free hand, she stuck the Sunbeam mixer into the potatoes and turned it on. The pot whirled around once, twice, and then spun right off the counter and onto the floor.

Chunks of potatoes whirled through the kitchen. Marty Joe started to laugh, smearing the potatoes through his hair and into his ears. I looked at Mom, and she looked as if she were about to cry.

"EDDIEEE!" she screamed at the top of her lungs. "EDDIE, HELP ME!!!"

Dad jerked his head up from the back of his La-Z-Boy and stammered, "What? . . . What, what is it, Florence?"

Mom hobbled over to the La-Z-Boy, her hair glued to her forehead with sweat. Ellen and I stood frozen at the end of the table. We looked at each other, then at Mom and back to Dad. Mom spoke slowly through clenched teeth, "Can, you, please, come, here, and, do *something*??"

"Like what, Flo?" Dad answered.

"Like, maybe, help, me, mash, the, damn, *potatoes!*"

"Florence," Dad replied, "you know that's not my job."

Dad picked up his pipe and Mom hopped back to the kitchen.

When Esther wrote the first check against our credit line, we discovered it had been pulled. Mr. Serling, our ex-friendly banker, had pulled it. He explained that credit lines were really for businesses that didn't need credit.

I knew something had to give, and it wasn't going to be Citibank.

Two silver-haired Italian men arrived at my office, dressed in dark gray hand-stitched suits, and introduced themselves as Mr. Vincent and Mr. Tony Albanese. They had built a new fifty-two-story condominium across from the United Nations and had blueprints rolled under their arms. They sat down in my small eleventh-floor office and the older brother, Vincent, commented on its neatness. "Small, but beautifully kept," he said.

The younger brother, Tony, seemed like the dealmaker. "My brother and I read your comments in yesterday's *Times*," he began, "and my brother and I are wondering if you'd be so kind as to tell us what you think our new condominium apartments could sell for."

"I'd be more than happy to, Mr. and Mr. Albanese," I replied, my mind warming at the thought of the commission on 250 apartments. "If you can take the time now to walk me through your blueprints, I can have prices for you by tomorrow."

When they left, I unrolled their floor plans and walked out to the sales area. "Linda," I interrupted a salesperson, "would you take a quick look at these apartment plans and give me your best guess as to what each might sell for?" Linda did, I wrote her initials next to each of her estimates, and then moved on to the next salesperson.

Forty-five minutes later, I had collected ten opinions. After averaging the prices for each of the six apartment sizes, I had a pretty good idea what the Albaneses' condominiums would sell for.

The two Albaneses arrived the next morning, and they seemed impressed by the neatly typed list of prices I had prepared. "Excellent work," Vincent congratulated me, as he examined the list of prices. "Excellent work!"

During the next few minutes of back-and-forth schmoozing, all I could think about was the $264,000 that I owed to my creditors. We needed cash and we needed it now. I decided to go for it.

"Mr. Albanese and Mr. Albanese, I've never in my entire life seen more beautiful floor plans than yours. They reflect the enormous thought you've obviously put into every detail. Your building's location is exceptional, your views the best in the city, and your black marble pyramid top is going to put the Empire State Building to shame! *I just love your building*, Mr. Albaneses, and I wonder if you would consider giving The Corcoran Group the honor of selling your property as your exclusive agent?" I bowed my head with respect and waited.

The brothers looked at each other, obviously impressed by my appreciation of their trophy property. It was Vincent who finally spoke, almost painfully. "Unfortunately, Miss Corcoran, I'm sorry to say that it's out of the question! Marty Raynes is a partner in our project and his company is already our exclusive agent."

I thought again about the $264,000. I thought about the credit line that got away. And I thought about this week's sales that only totaled two.

I smiled my most innocent smile.

"Well, how about sales manager?" I asked, trying to disguise my desperation as enthusiasm.

Tony smiled like a kindly godfather, and asked, "But why would *you*, Miss Corcoran, want to work as a sales manager when you're the president of this successful operation?"

"Because I could learn so much working for you and your

brother," I explained. Tony seemed satisfied with my answer and leaned back.

Vincent, however, was suspicious, squinting his eyes and pursuing the question further. "I think that might be a conflict of interest," he said. "Let's say, Miss Corcoran, that one of your salespeople brought in a customer who bought one of our condos. We would owe your company a full five percent commission. How could I be sure that that customer didn't come into our building first, and that you didn't refer him to one of your salespeople just to get the commission?"

At that, I spread my hand over my heart and gasped. I remembered my "almost a nun" statement that had worked so well years earlier with Mr. Campagna, my landlord who wanted to evict me. I decided right then to take the story one step further.

"Mr. Albaneses, *that* would be impossible! Why, I'm a former nun!"

I started work with the respectful Italian Albanese brothers one week later for an annual salary of $200,000. I planned to use half of my new salary to pay Esther so that she could give up sales and be in the office full-time. I'd use the other $100,000 to keep ahead on our advertising bill. If we couldn't advertise, we'd be out of business.

In the second week on my new job, a sophisticated Italian woman arrived at the condominium sales office. She looked a lot like Sophia Loren, and I knew she was "a ringer," a spy to test my integrity. She might as well have been carrying a sign.

"I've beena working, witha Eleanora, froma The Corcoran Groupa," she tolda mea. "Do I needa, hera, to showa-mea, thesa condos?"

"Why, that's not necessary at all," I replied. "I'll take you up to see the condos right now." She didn't buy a condo, but I had honored my vows and passed the Albanese integrity test.

* * *

I thought back to my memory of my mother quietly hopping back to the kitchen as my dad sat in his La-Z-Boy. Mom's unspoken words still burned in my memory: "In a family, *everyone helps mash the potatoes.*"

For the next six months, I fed my after-tax income back to The Corcoran Group, paying our bills and buying more time.

✳

MOM'S LESSON #17: In a family, everyone helps mash the potatoes.

✳

THE LESSON LEARNED ABOUT HELPING OUT

By moonlighting for the Albanese brothers, I earned the needed cash that bought my struggling company some time. And I discovered that the new job gave me the opportunity to learn something new, and through that job, I learned a lot about marketing new developments. That knowledge would later lead to the opening of a new marketing division for The Corcoran Group.

My willingness to go out and take a second job to keep us afloat set an example that was noticed by everyone at the company. Because I was willing to personally put myself on the line, everyone at The Corcoran Group rallied around the flag and pitched in. They formed listing teams, taught workshops, helped each other negotiate, supported cuts in advertising, and even took pay cuts.

Nothing is more powerful than a team working together. Teams can accomplish anything, but to create an exceptional team, the members must totally believe that *no one of us is as smart as all of us.*

18

Moms Can't Quit

December 1990. The Corcoran Group.

Every time the office door opened, I looked up from my desk with dread. I was petrified that someone would walk in with a big dolly and walk out with our furniture. I hadn't taken a salary from the business in months and with the help of a friendly mortgage broker had put a $450,000 mortgage on my $350,000 country house. That money was already spent so I sold my third-floor one-bedroom condo on East Sixty-third and moved one block down into an illegal sublet, a rent-controlled walk-up on East Sixty-second Street, which was leased by my cousin.

My new apartment came with a pet, the biggest cockroach in New York City, and he lived in my bathtub. When I got home at night, he was there waiting for me, wiggling his two antennae back and forth above the drain. I surprised myself by taking a liking to him, and soon considered him my pet.

In recent months, the only phone ringing belonged to Sylvia, my secretary-bookkeeper, and she had clearly become the most popular person at the office. She answered one call after another from suppliers, offering small goodwill payments in exchange for a little more time.

Esther suggested I use her personal savings to keep the business afloat, and one of my nicest salespeople, Edith, quietly offered me her husband's pension fund. But not knowing if I would be able to pay either back, I declined. I felt bad enough owing our creditors money, never mind owing money to people I personally knew.

I went over our bills and receivables once more. We were clearly in the red, blood red, and for the first time, I faced the fact that we were going out of business.

I unplugged the office Christmas tree, turned off the lights, and headed home through the holiday hustle of Madison Avenue. I needed to find the right words to tell everyone I was closing the business, but I figured I could wait two weeks until after the holidays.

Friday night. The Corcoran kitchen.

"I quit!" Mom declared to no one as the kitchen filled with smoke, and she clanged the smoking black pan of charred flounder into the sink. She stomped over to Dad's La-Z-Boy, and handed Mary Jean off with a curt, "She's wet, change her!"

The next time we saw Mom it was almost six o'clock. We were milling around the kitchen when she appeared in her full Sunday dress, hat and all. Nana was standing on her right, and her blue Samsonite suitcase was at the ready on her left.

"I'm leaving!" she announced loudly.

"What about dinner?" Eddie asked.

"Your father's in charge. Ask him!" she said, picking up her suitcase and heading toward the front door.

We all ran to the front window to watch Mom ka-thump her suitcase down the front steps, jerk it up onto the sidewalk, and head down Hilliard Avenue. We watched as Mom dragged her suitcase past Gene's Candy Store, Mrs. Mertz's bakery, Bernie Beck's supermarket, and as she went over the ridge by Uncle Dick's police station, we couldn't see Mom anymore.

Mom plunked herself down on the green wooden bench at the bus stop on River Road and waited. She didn't know where she was going, she was just going. With a household full of kids, Mom was tired of being the full-time repairman, laundress, nurse, tutor, and cook. But the final straw that Friday night was that Dad wasn't helping her get us ready for his cousin's wedding the next day in Toms River.

As she waited for the number 8 bus to New York, a handsome, well-dressed man with a leather attaché case sat down next to her. Mom yanked the two pink sponge curlers from her bangs. When the bus arrived, Mom paid her fare, took a seat at the front of the bus, and the handsome man sat down beside her. "Going my way?" he whispered to my mother.

It was two blocks south at the stop in front of the Edgewater Aluminum Factory that Mom grabbed her suitcase and ran out of the bus.

We were all sitting at the dinner table, pushing Nana's frozen fish sticks around our plates, when Mom appeared in the kitchen. "I'm home," she said to no one, and plunked her suitcase down.

We looked up at Mom and waited. John was the first to ask, "Where'd you go, Mom?"

"To the aluminum factory and back," she said, taking off her hat.

"But Dad said you quit," Ellen added, taking a quick look at Dad.

Mom sat down, sprinkled some peas onto Mary Jean's tray, and said, "Moms can't quit."

After trying everything to keep my business afloat, I returned to the office on January 2, and received one of the most challenging and timely phone calls of my life.

*

MOM'S LESSON #18: Moms can't quit.

*

THE LESSON LEARNED
ABOUT *NOT* QUITTING

I find that every big success happens after I think I've exhausted 100 percent of my options. For me, success only happened *after* I gave another 10 percent.

19

When There Are Ten Buyers and Three Puppies, Every Dog Is the Pick of the Litter

Early January, 1991.

"Where's the kitchen?" I asked as the superintendent opened the door to yet another dreadful apartment.

"This one doesn't have one," he said, "but the pipes are all there."

I had already scheduled the sales meeting to announce the closing of the business when a big developer called and asked that I appraise a group of eighty-eight apartments in six buildings that he and his financial partners owned on the Upper East and West Sides. The apartments were leftovers from the go-go years, before the real estate market did a jackknife dive, ending with a splat.

Bernie Mendik and his investment partner, Equitable Insurance, had a $50 million underlying mortgage on the buildings, leaving each apartment's monthly maintenance charge 40 percent higher than the rest of the market. The high maintenance, along with the difficulty buyers were having in finding financing, made the apartments virtually impossible to sell.

I looked at the white-tile, white-tub, white-sinked bathroom badly in need of caulking. "At least there's a bathroom. It's lovely!" I commented, and closed the door.

Finding buyers for these apartments would be no easy feat. Prices had plummeted 40 percent since the stock market crashed in '87 and every would-be customer in New York City still believed that if they waited, they'd be able to buy any apartment for less the following day.

I returned to the office and called Mr. Mendik. "I'm afraid I have bad news, Bernie," I began. "There's just no way your apartments can be sold in this market. They've been listed for more than three years and there aren't any takers. I'm sure you're aware that the apartments need a ton of work and the maintenance charges are way out of line with the rest of the market. I'm sorry, Bernie, I really wish I could help."

"Barbara," Bernie responded with his trademark enthusiasm, "you're a smart girl! You'll figure it out." And he hung up the phone.

Summer. Toms River.

Grandpa Ward was a huge man with big hands who lived in a small clapboard cabin in Toms River, New Jersey. To visit him, we took the two-hour trip sardine-style in the back of Dad's Blue Beauty station wagon. Grandpa Ward's house was at the end of a long dirt road, which he shared with the chicken farm across the way.

When we arrived, Grandpa had already prepared the usual lunch of warmed canned beets that he insisted were rich in iron and would make my brothers "strong, strappin' men." My sisters and I quietly wondered if women got strappin' too, and if not, why did *we* have to eat them?

We were sitting outside on Grandpa's screened porch after lunch when I heard a lot of noise at the farm across the road. "MOM!" I yelled with my hands cupped on the screen door, "there's some fancy cars pulling up to the farm. Can we go see what's going on?"

"Just a minute," she answered, "and we'll all go together. Ellen, help me finish the dishes, and, Denise, put away the cups. John, sit on Grandpa's lap there and, Eddie, wipe your face. Barbara, stay right there, and, keep your eye on Tommy, Mary, Martin, and Jeanine."

By the time we got to the road, there was a line of fancy cars, and a line of fancy city folks to go with them waited by the gate.

"What's going on today?" my mother asked a lady in a very shiny dress.

"What's going on?" the lady repeated, flapping a fan in front of her face. "What's going on is that that farmer lady gave me an appointment at noon and then let *that* woman there ahead of me."

"I had an appointment at noon, too," grumbled the bald-headed man behind her.

"And so did *we*," a very skinny lady said, standing with a man by their blue convertible. "And, by the way," the very skinny lady added, "you're behind *us*."

"Oh, I don't have an appointment," my mother explained, as she straightened the hem of her housedress. "We're just visiting our relatives next door."

"What's everyone waiting for?" Denise asked.

"For the puppies," the lady with the fan said as if we should know. "They're Jack Russells, and they have three of them for sale right over there next to the barn."

"You better make that *two*," a lady with a poufed head of blond hair said as she walked past cradling a tiny brown-spotted puppy. She was making baby sounds. "I got the absolutely cutest one of all! Just look at his sweet little face!"

The people waiting in line bristled, and Mom moved us out of the way as the line squeezed closer together. "Come over here, kids," she directed, as the fan lady hurried through the gate, "and I'll tell you what's really going on." Mom laughed to herself as she explained: "The farmer's wife was smart enough to get everyone to come at the same time because she knew it would make everyone want a puppy!"

"But why would it make everyone want a puppy, Mom?" Ellen asked.

"Because everybody wants what everybody wants. And when there are ten buyers and only three puppies, every dog becomes the pick of the litter."

I had an idea! What was good for the puppies would be good for apartments. The next day, I called Bernie back to make an appointment. Bernie liked my new idea and asked me to explain it to his partners later that week, which I did. Next, I explained it to three serious men from the underwriting banks. And later explained it to the even *more* serious men from the lead lender, Chase Manhattan Bank. And finally I explained it to the *most* serious men of all from the Equitable Life Insurance Society of the United States, the majority investor. They all seriously liked it.

By the fifteenth of January, my last-ditch plan to save my business was in full swing.

"Here's how it works," I said to Esther and to one of my best agents, Tresa Hall. Tresa had agreed to be the project's sales manager. "I've priced all the studios at $49,500, all the one-bedrooms at $99,500, and all the two-bedrooms at $165,500."

"Even the high floors?" Esther interrupted.

"Yes, high floors, low floors, front apartments and back apartments, *all priced the same*. Apartments with views or no views, those with new kitchens, old kitchens, or no kitchens at all, all priced the same!"

"But how's that possible?" Esther asked.

"I added up all of the original asking prices, divided by the number of units in each building, and then deducted ten percent, because that's what people would have negotiated off the price anyway."

Esther shifted slightly in her chair.

"And I've also taken away every objection that a buyer could possibly have. There's no board approval needed and one of the banks with a big stake in the buildings has agreed to provide the mortgages. Also, there'll be no monthly maintenance charges *for two whole years*! None!"

"*None?*" Tresa repeated. "But that's crazy! Who'll pay the maintenance each month?"

"The sellers will," I answered, "because it's included in the sale price. We're simply giving the buyers one less check to write each month and moving the high-maintenance objection out of the way." I pulled out a sample contract and continued, "We'll have the eighty-eight contracts prepared in advance by the seller's attorney, and we'll stack them high for everyone to see. The buyers will sign them right then and there the morning of the sale."

"But that isn't legal, is it?" Esther queried, as she tilted her head to the left. "Barbara, you know buyers have to show the contract to their attorney before they can sign it!"

I pulled out the big rubber stamp I had had made and with one quick motion imprinted the sample contract on my desk with bold lettering:

CONSULT YOUR ATTORNEY.
YOU HAVE *TWO WEEKS* FROM THIS DATE
TO CANCEL THE CONTRACT AND
RECEIVE YOUR FULL DEPOSIT BACK.

Esther and Tresa looked cautiously optimistic.

* * *

At the next Monday meeting, I announced to our salespeople that we had eighty-eight new co-op apartments for sale, that they were located in six different buildings on the Upper East and West Sides, and that we were going to sell all of the apartments on the same day for the same price. "Pick any studio for $49,500," I said emphatically, "any one-bedroom for $99,500, or any two-bedroom for $165,500!"

When I wouldn't disclose the apartments' addresses, everyone wanted to know where they were even more. "This is not a sale open to *everyone* and it will *not* be advertised." I had no money for advertising, but didn't share that fact. "We will distribute the exact addresses and unit numbers *only* on the morning of the sale. I ask that you please tell only, I repeat *only*, your very best customers. And, of course, you can also tell your family. The sale is limited to *one per customer* and will take place three weeks from today, first-come, first-served. Nine A.M. sharp!"

Everyone looked intrigued, and after I ended the meeting, I could still hear the buzz from my office.

Two weeks before the day of the sale, I added fuel to the fire by worrying aloud to a few salespeople, "I'm a little concerned that we might not have enough to go around." My whisper campaign created a virtual frenzy.

A week before the sale, accusations began to fly that someone had gotten hold of "The List" and that she was already telling her customers which apartments were the best ones. I quelled the rumor at that Monday's meeting.

"No one has the list!" I stated emphatically to the crowded sales floor. "I repeat, No one has the list! There's *only one list*, and it's safely locked in Esther Kaplan's drawer. Esther, please show them!" With that, Esther played magician's assistant and walked over to her desk, where she unlocked the drawer and pulled out the sheets of typed paper. As she held them up and turned from one side of the room to the other, fifty salespeople wiggled forward for a better view.

"Thank you, Esther." I nodded. "Now, please lock it back up!" Everyone watched as Esther put the list into an envelope, put the envelope in the drawer, locked it, and dropped the key into her purse. "*Everyone* will get the list next Monday morning, nine A.M. sharp!"

8:55 A.M. East Sixty-ninth Street.

"Stand back!" Tresa Hall, a former flight attendant, commanded the chaotic, shoving throng of buyers. "I repeat, stand back and clear the doors!"

I was shocked to see the crowd of buyers stretching to the end of the block. "Excuse me, excuse me, please, excuse me," I repeated as I made my way up East Sixty-ninth Street.

The line had started at 4:00 A.M., and by 8:30 had grown to include hundreds of people desperate to snag an apartment. Tresa's voice cut through the crowd. "We will distribute the list of apartments momentarily," she said, demonstrating with broad flight attendant arm motions. "And we'll be handing it out starting in the front and will work our way to the back of the line as quickly as possible. Please note that a map is attached to the back of each list with all the addresses and apartment numbers clearly marked. There are salespeople stationed on every floor in each of the buildings, the apartment doors are open, so that you can go in and look at any apartment you choose. Once you've made your decision, however, you must return to *this* table in *this* lobby to sign the contract." She directed all eyes toward the banquet table, which stood in the lobby with eighty-eight waiting contracts stacked high.

"When you are ready to sign a contract and leave us your ten percent deposit check, the apartment will be *immediately* taken off the market. Please have several apartments you'd like to try for, as your first choice may already be taken! You'll be given a copy of the signed contract to take with you for your attorney.

"Okay, then," Tresa finished, and with great ceremony said,

"we'll now hand out the list of apartments!" The crowd inched forward and I wondered if I should have hired a few uniformed policemen to protect her, or at least for dramatic effect.

Like a Macy's Day Sale without the clothes, people began to run the moment the list was in their hands. In the mayhem, everyone had a strategy for charting, hunting, darting, looking, rushing, signing, and buying. Some people waited on elevators, while others bolted for the stairs. Some worked alone, while others worked in pairs.

The first successful buyer had flown in from Paris and had camped in line since 4:00 in the morning. He signed a contract for a one-bedroom on the highest floor, sight unseen, six blocks away.

One savvy couple had a pair of cellular phones and were calling each other back and forth as they dashed through the buildings looking at apartments. It was the first day I saw cell phones in use. When they decided on an apartment they liked, the husband ran to the table while his wife kept looking, just in case. As he signed the contract, he called his wife on her cellular and said, "Honey, we got one, you can stop."

One man rushed back to the contract table announcing he liked the C line of apartments in the building. "It doesn't matter which floor, I just want to buy a C, any C." When we told him that all the C's had been sold, he decided he liked B's, too, "any B."

We started the day with eighty-eight apartments that nobody wanted and our company near bankruptcy. By day's end, eighty-eight proud new owners were celebrating their good fortune, and we had eighty-eight checks to deposit and had earned over a million dollars in net commissions.

❋

MOM'S LESSON #19: When there are ten buyers and three puppies, *every* dog is the pick of the litter.

❋

THE LESSON LEARNED
ABOUT MARKETING

On the morning of our One Day Sale, the economy was in a slump and New York City real estate prices were down. But the market was ready to come back, if only someone would prime the pump. Our "eighty-eight-sales-in-a-day" was its wake-up call.

The One Day Sale was a great marketing gambit, but it was *not* a swindle. It was a fair deal, and its easy terms enabled people previously unable to buy an apartment to do so. It was also a good deal for the sellers because it enabled them to make more money than they would if they sold the apartments at auction.

When the last apartment sold, there were still another fifty buyers who wished they had gotten one. One guy who didn't get an apartment actually sued us, saying the couple who used cell phones cheated. We settled the suit by selling him the next apartment that became available.

As a result of the One Day Sale, I learned five big lessons about marketing.

1. **Everybody wants what everybody wants.**
   Competition always communicates the message that there's a good deal to be had. And when people are told that they can't have something, they want it even more.

   On the day of the One Day Sale, buyers could plainly see the number of customers ahead of them and behind them in line. Even the customers who weren't sure they wanted an apartment decided they wanted one as the litter thinned.

   By announcing the sale date in advance, we set the stage with anticipation. The "one per customer" rule emphasized the fact that there was a limited supply, and the pile of contracts, waiting on the banquet table, added to the sales pressure.

None of the buyers bailed out, because they knew there were another fifty people in line behind them who went home empty-handed.

2. **Create a deadline and you create urgency.**
As long as customers perceive the value as fair, urgency can be created by setting a deadline. Our offer to "pick any one-bedroom for the *same price*" created urgency as customers raced to pick the best one. And as most people buy with their hearts and justify with their heads, our "sign now/think later" strategy felt acceptable, even though it was contrary to the way business was usually done.

3. **The biggest opportunities abound when nothing else is going on.**
Most people are afraid to step up to the plate when no one else is around. The apartments sold at the One Day Sale had languished on the market for three years. They were sold at the bottom of the real estate cycle.

In marketing, all my biggest opportunities were always found in the silences. I've learned to look hard at the silences.

4. **The best time to answer an objection is before it's raised.**
At the One Day Sale, we addressed all the buyers' potential objections *up front*. As most of the customers were first-time buyers, the prospect of securing a co-op board approval was frightening. So we eliminated it.

In New York, real estate contracts are usually prepared by the seller's attorney and then take two to five weeks of legal review before signing. We said, "Sign now, show it to your attorney later." The oversized legal warning stamped on the front of the contract made the buyers comfortable enough to sign. Finally, by paying the first two years' maintenance charges out of the proceeds of the sale, we positioned the property's biggest liability as a plus. And as the market rebounded, the price appreciation more than offset the high maintenance fees.

5. **Taking chances almost always makes for happy endings.**
   And did the buyers *really* get a good deal? The studios they bought in 1991 for $49,500 sell today for $220,000, the one-bedrooms they bought for $99,500 sell today for $400,000, and the two-bedrooms bought for $165,000 now sell for $700,000. Eighty-eight lucky buyers all with happy endings.

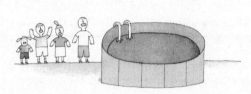

20

Jumping Out the Window Will Make You Either an Ass or a Hero

1993. The Corcoran Group.

For the first time in a long time, I had ended the previous year with a profit, a clear $71,000 after-tax profit, and it was burning a hole in my pocket. I knew God had put that money in my hand for some divine purpose, and I had decided to spend all of it on my new video idea.

My idea seemed surefire. First, I hired a photographer to take pictures of our listings, seventy-three, to be exact, and put all of them on videotape. The videos were categorized by number of bedrooms and showed everything in each apartment—the floor plans, the building's lobby, the rooms and even the views outside their windows, and each listing description ended with a photo and the phone number of the listing salesperson. I even hired a professional makeup artist so our salespeople would look their very best.

I couldn't wait to introduce my new idea at the companywide sales meeting! I stood at the lit podium in front of my two hundred or so salespeople and bragged, "Our new video will give our Corcoran Group customers *all the information* they could possibly want. All in one convenient place! We're calling it *Homes on Tape. HOT* for short. Get it? Now, thanks to this innovation, our customers can shop for apartments anywhere, anytime, simply by picking up a copy of our video at any of our offices and taking it home for only a twenty-dollar, fully refundable deposit. It's just perfect for the busy New Yorker!"

As I raised my arms into a high papal V, I vowed, "Our *Homes on Tape* will transform the way people buy and sell real estate forever! Now, New Yorkers will be able to see all the property they want, without ever having to leave their own couch! Amen!"

The entire sales team burst into spontaneous applause as I dramatically nodded my head and lowered my arms. *Yep*, I thought, *this is my best idea yet!*

Summer. The side yard.

Marty Joe was perched on the third-story window ledge outside the girls' room, grinning from ear to ear. *"We're ready!"* we all shouted up.

Marty's legs looked white against his navy-blue swim trunks high above our heads. He was about to leap out over the Roanes' landing into the plastic-walled, blue metal-framed pool Dad and Grandpa had set up in the side yard. The pool was four feet deep, but was a lot shallower next to the house, where Dad and Grandpa couldn't make it level against the hill.

"Are you sure you're ready?" Marty shouted down. For a moment, I thought he looked nervous, maybe even scared, but, then again, Marty Joe was the kid who would try anything.

"Come on, let's *go*, Marty Joe!" Jimmy Cleary called up.

"Do it, Dart!" another kid added.

My brother Marty had more nicknames than any other member of our family. He was baptized Martin Joseph, which was shortened to Marty Joe. Later, the kids in the neighborhood named him Martin

Jartin. That lasted until the summer day when he demonstrated his technique for throwing a dart in the air and catching it by its tail. Blinded by the glare of the sun, he missed a dart as it shot back to earth, and it landed squarely between his eyes.

The other kids' excited cries, as they watched him run in circles like a chicken without a head, were music to Marty's attention-loving ears.

"Look at me!" he shouted to the crowd like the sideshow barker at the amusement park. "Look at me, the aa-maaaazing 'Martin *Dart*in,' pierced by a flying dart that went straight to his *braaaaaaaain!*"

With the bloody dart poking from his forehead like a bull's-eye shot on a dartboard, Marty took a bow to mixed applause and shrieks of horror. His self-anointed name stuck, and Martin Jartin became forever known as Martin Dartin, or "Dart" for short.

"Dart," Michael Mertz shouted up with his hands cupped like a megaphone, "we don't have all day!"

With that, Martin Dartin leapt off the window ledge, sailed past Mrs. Roane's landing, and hurtled toward the shallow section of our plastic pool.

"What an asshole!" my brother Eddie shouted, as we all scrambled away from the pool with a collective gasp. We all covered our eyes as Marty plunged into the water. When we opened them, Marty was standing up in the middle of the pool bowing and everyone ran and crowded around the pool.

"I don't believe it! I don't believe it! I just don't believe it," we all clamored, congratulating Marty for being alive.

Marty looked as amazed by his survival as we were. Shaking the water from his hair, he reached out for the hands of his adoring fan club.

"Hey, what's happening?" Stevie Mertz hollered as he hurdled the front retaining wall. "What's going on, what did I miss?"

"Dart just jumped off the roof and lived!" Timmy Tom proudly exclaimed as he inched closer to Marty, trying to catch some of his glow.

"And he hit the pool dead center!" Ellen bragged.

"Oh, man," Stevie whined, "but I didn't see it. That's a bummer."

Without a moment's thought, Marty gripped the pool's edge, swung his muscular legs between his arms, and popped out of the pool dripping wet. "No problem!" Marty said. "Watch me this time, I'll do it again."

Before Marty's second jump ended, he had become the town hero.

That night, while Mom pounded the chicken cutlets, we were all still talking about Marty's amazing feat. Mom didn't look happy. She rolled out a sheet of waxed paper, looked up at Marty, and said, "Jumping out that window could have made you either an ass *or* a hero. You got *lucky*, Marty." As Dad came in the front door from work, Mom lowered her voice. "Since your father's interpretation won't match your friends'," she warned, pointing with the meat cleaver, "you better keep your braggin' to yourself."

December 1993. Corcoran West Side.

I made my way down the wooden steps that leaned precariously against the moldy cinder-block wall in the wet basement of our West Side office, right next door to Zabar's deli on Broadway.

I pulled the string on the single lightbulb at the bottom of the stairs, and it cast a dull yellow light over the final resting place of my $71,000 investment. Thirty-two piles of black video boxes were stacked eight feet high against the back wall. My *Homes on Tape* idea was dead on arrival, and not one person came to "check out" our video sales tour.

My brilliant marketing innovation had a pair of Achilles' heels. First, our salespeople didn't give out the videos because they didn't want to show customers another salesperson's face or phone number. Second, the videos contained so many images that each shot clicked on and off faster than even the New York eye could possibly see.

I glared at the eight-foot pile of videos sucking up the water from the basement floor and knew I should be giving some serious thought to how to recoup the $71,000 I had blown on my big idea. But, instead, all I could think about was the next big sales meeting and how stupid I would look standing there in front of everyone explaining why my great idea had belly-flopped.

I climbed back up the basement stairs and headed over to the East Side, where I was meeting my husband at Maxwell's Plum for dinner. A former FBI agent and a captain in the naval reserves, Wild Bill Higgins had just returned from three weeks of war games with the U.S. Navy in South Korea. He was anxious to tell me about his trip, and, between big bites of steak, he excitedly gestured and explained how he had played war games against North Korea on computer. He was a lot more animated than usual.

"It was incredible, Barb, you should have seen it! We fought the whole war on this new thing called the Internet, and it was exactly like a *real war*. We were moving our ships and supplies as if there was really a war going on!"

I was still bruised by the soggy image of my pile of tapes and was trying my best to feign interest. I took another sip of my white wine and said, "Didn't you play those same games last year in Washington?" I asked.

"It was totally different, Barb." He chewed on. "We were actually playing war in *real time*. When the North Koreans bombed us, we immediately bombed them back. And when they took out our ports and highways, we instantly blew up their supply ships. You could see everything on the computer like it was actually happening!"

"Well, who won?" I asked, hoping to conclude and move on to my subject.

He smiled. "*They* did!" he said. "And the South Koreans went berserk! You'd think they had actually lost a war." He gestured with his fork. "We had to keep reminding them that it was just a game on a computer!"

"Is the Internet thing only in the navy?" I asked. "Made to play war games?"

"No, Barb, that's just it, it's not just for games. Anyone can use it to exchange any information with anyone, anywhere, anytime, as long as they have a computer. And it's free! I'm telling you, Barb, this World Wide Web is going to connect everybody and become the greatest library of instant information on the planet!"

The following week, my salesperson Linda Stillwell volunteered to have her husband in the computer business register our company's "domain" name on his computer. Then I hired the video guy to put our *Homes on Tape* pictures on the World Wide Web.

January 1994.

"Ladies and gentlemen, today I'm proud to announce phase two of our *Homes on Tape* video project! The Corcoran Group will be one of the first companies in America to take our listings into cyberspace!" Although I didn't know if anyone besides the South Koreans could *find* our listings there, I knew for sure that I had come up with a plan to save face. Everyone applauded.

Within the month, four new customers found our properties on the World Wide Web, and my belly-flop began to look like a heroic leap into the future.

✳

MOM'S LESSON #20: Jumping out the window will make you either an ass or a hero.

✳

THE LESSON LEARNED ABOUT INNOVATION

I've found that all innovation is built on a leap and a prayer using money you shouldn't have spent in the first place, and that waiting to spend money on a good idea is the business equivalent of saving the good china for Sunday.

Here are my personal beliefs about all innovation:

1. **People are reluctant to innovate.**

   It's *not* because they don't have good ideas, it's simply because they don't enjoy failing. The best innovators are great at failing. They might look like they're flying, but four times out of five they're simply falling with style.

2. **There's no better time to bring a good idea to life than at the moment of its inception.**

   The surest way to kill a good idea is to send it to a committee.

3. **Anyone can have a good idea, but it's a rare person who can make the good ideas happen.**

4. **The "Big Idea" rarely comes from top management.**

   Most great ideas come from the little guy, told to the big guy who listens.

5. Innovation never happens in a dictatorship.
    Period.

6. Nothing new was ever invented without a lot of flops.
    The best way to justify spending money on a new business idea
    is to categorize it as "research and development."

The first four customers who visited our Web site were only the beginning of the coming wave. In 1993, the world had only fifty Web
sites, and by the time we started corcoran.com one year later, there
were already several hundred. Today there are more than 7 million
Web sites, and corcoran.com generates more than $700 million a
year in sales.

Here's how I've used the Internet to build my business:

1. The idea is to be first.
    When it comes to the Web, I never try to be perfect, I try to be
    first. Our company was the first to put floor plans on our Web
    site and the first to introduce virtual tours, market appraisals,
    broker profiles, neighborhood mapping, and chat rooms. None
    of our ideas were original; they were just original to our industry.

2. Have lunch or be lunch.
    I've initiated more good things on the Internet simply because I
    was afraid my competitor would do them if I didn't.

3. The little guy has the advantage.
    Small businesses can be more creative and move faster than
    larger businesses on the Internet. The online medium thrives on
    creativity and speed. The Web is also a great equalizer because it
    lets the little guy *appear* to be as large as the big one.

4. **Be prepared to spend a lot more money than you expect.**
   Whatever you think the cost will be to develop your new technology, triple it. Why? Because the Internet is a moving target
   that will always offer a better software option the following
   month. And after your Web site is built, it has to be constantly
   adapted and improved for future use.

5. **Buy the software off the shelf.**
   Inevitably, someone has already developed a software program
   that can be tailored to your needs. Develop your own software
   only as an absolute last resort.

6. **Beware of technology people who look like leprechauns.**
   They weave a magical story, sprinkle it with fairy dust, empty your
   pockets, and, *poof!*, disappear into the forest. They speak a secret
   language you're not meant to understand, like "the right business
   model," which means "wishful thinking," and "beta testing,"
   which means "we're not ready yet." And "burn rate" is exactly
   what it sounds like. Don't hire them. Find people who can understand your business and explain in practical terms what needs to
   be done.

7. **Use the Internet to build loyal customers.**
   Customers love the anonymity and control the Internet gives
   them. When a customer finds you on the Web, the relationship
   quickly moves from voyeur to pen pal to "friend for life," faster
   than it does through any other medium. And when the customer
   finally meets you, they are more loyal than any other.

8. **Make your information two clicks away.**
   Consumers consistently cite "ease of use" as their number one
   reason for choosing a Web site. More than two clicks is one click
   too many.

9. **Put your URL on everything.**
   The best way to promote your online brand is through your off-line marketing. Put your URL on everything you print and make sure it's as big as your company's name.

10. **Online Internet advertising doesn't work.**
    Don't be fooled. Online advertising is cheap for a reason. It simply doesn't work.

The Corcoran Group became known as the industry innovator because we grabbed every small opportunity along the way to initiate change. In short, we were consistently willing to jump out the window.

DO'S AND DON'TS OF EFFECTIVE E-MAIL

We all get a lot of e-mail, and like other forms of communication, there are always ways to do it better.

1. Don't use e-mail as a way to avoid speaking with people. Speaking with someone reveals and invokes more information than e-mail ever will.
2. Keep it short and sweet. Short, clear e-mails show respect for the recipient's time, but terse one or two word responses convey, "I have no time for you."
3. Always use a descriptive subject heading to increase your chances of being read.
4. Salutations like: "Hi Barbara" give a personal touch when writing to individuals.
5. Don't write in all capital letters as it's the e-mail equivalent of SHOUTING.
6. Always sphelchek!
7. Billboard yourself with an automatic "see my web page" link.

8. Don't hit the send button right away. Instead, save a draft and come back to it. It will help you be more clear, and protects you from saying something you'll regret later.

9. Don't spam. Spammers are the annoying computer equivalent to telemarketers.

10. Don't send chain letters or unnecessary large attachments. No one likes them.

11. Learn the most useful e-mail features like automatic signature, Out-of-Office Assistant, and automatic distribution lists. Learn the difference between clicking "Reply," "Reply to All," and "Forward."

12. Set your program for the subject line to be presented first, so you can delete e-mails without having to open them.

13. Categorize and colorize your groups to make it easy to prioritize importance and order of response. For example, personal correspondence can appear in red and go into a red inbox, business contacts appear in green and go into a green inbox, etc.

14. Unless you're in business for yourself, don't use your work e-mail address for personal communication of a sensitive nature. To avoid problems with the boss, maintain a separate address.

21

You Have the Right
to Be There

December 1993. The Corcoran Group.

It all started when Sylvia, my assistant, bustled into my office, her feathers obviously ruffled. "She says her name is Susan Cara and she's one of our salespeople," Sylvia puffed, "but *I've* never seen her before, and she doesn't even have an appointment!"

"That's okay, Sylvia," I said, smoothing down her feathers. "Just show her in."

Susan Cara had the best legs I'd ever seen on *anyone*. She clicked over to my desk in heels so high I got ready to catch her if she tripped. The micro-mini she wore was a half-inch too short and I could see she didn't have stockings on. She tugged her skirt down as she slid into the chair across from my desk and grinned, the tip of her tongue resting on her two front teeth.

"It's nice to meet you, Susan," I said. "You must be one of our new brokers."

"I'm not new," she quickly corrected me.

"I'm sorry," I apologized. "I haven't met you before, so I assumed you were new. How long have you been here?"

"Three weeks."

"Three weeks," I repeated. "Well, I guess that seems like a long time." I settled in for what I knew was going to be an interesting conversation. "So, how can I help you?"

Susan crossed her legs once and then again in the other direction. "I have an investor," she started, "and he wants to buy big hotels in New York."

"Oh, that's good news," I said. "I can certainly help you with that. I'll call the two largest commercial firms and get you the name of their best broker who specializes in hotel sales. Who's your customer, Susan?"

"A conglomerate," she answered abruptly.

"Okay, then, Susan," I said, "you don't have to give me the name, but you should know that you'll have to give *them* your customer's name if you want to collect a referral commission. They'll probably pay you twenty or maybe even twenty-five percent of their commission, and on a hotel sale that could be sizable."

Susan leaned forward in her seat. "No," she said firmly. "I plan to sell them myself."

"Susan, although I can appreciate that, you've only been with us for three weeks, so you might not know that the commercial sales business is a whole different kettle of fish than residential sales. Our company sells apartments and town houses, because that's our expertise. I'm afraid you'd be doing yourself, our company, and, most important, your *customer* a disservice if you tried to help them yourself. But if you refer them, you'll have the best two commercial firms in New York working for your customer."

"Thank you." She smiled and left my office to go out and totally ignore my advice.

* * *

"I'm telling you, Barbara, this lady is going to get us in trouble," Susan's sales manager fretted to me by phone. "She's calling every big hotel owner in town, asking them to sell their property to her mystery client, and leaving a wake of complaints in her path. She has absolutely no idea what she's talking about, and she won't listen. I think you should do something about her, Barbara, because everything about her spells trouble."

Susan's manager told me she had hired her because Susan was very aggressive and seemed eager to learn. But within her few short weeks at the company, she had succeeded in alienating the entire office; the others saw her as different and resented her know-it-all attitude.

Her manager reported that Susan wasn't interested in learning her real estate ABCs. She knew exactly what she wanted, which was to jump from A to Z. And she got lucky by snagging a big conglomerate referral when she listed her own house for sale in Brooklyn.

I waited two days to get an appointment, and when she finally prowled into my office, it was clear to me that I was either going to have to fire her or let her do exactly as she pleased.

"So, Susan, how's it going?" I pleasantly inquired.

"I want you to call Donald Trump for me," she answered. "My client wants to buy the Plaza Hotel."

"Ohkaaay," I said. "But you need to tell me something about your client, Susan."

"Like what?" she asked.

"Like where he's from," I said.

"Hong Kong," she aggressively snapped back.

"And *who* exactly are they?" I persisted.

"A conglomerate."

"Listen, Susan, I need to know more than that. I'll need to know that they're legitimate buyers before I can make any calls for you."

"They're for real," she stated conclusively, looking around the room as if I were wasting her time.

At the last toss of her hair, I was beginning to relish the thought of firing her. I leaned back in my chair, trying to arrive at the right solution.

I tried to put my dislike for Susan aside and had to acknowledge that anyone who was so dogged in holding on to a client probably *did* have a big fish on the end of the line. And by witnessing how aggressive she was, I figured she would somehow find a way to reel it in.

But I knew I couldn't have Susan running around town alienating the commercial property owners and risking my reputation in the process. Susan was way out of her league. She didn't know a damn thing about selling commercial property. In fact, Susan and The Corcoran Group had no right whatsoever dabbling in someone else's market.

Spring. Chicky Dayock's house.

"Barbara Ann," Mom said, "Chicky Dayock is a very nice woman, and you have nothing to be afraid of. Besides," she added as she put the stuffed peppers into the oven and slammed the door shut, "you have just as much right as anybody else to win that thousand dollars."

"But what do I have to do?" I asked, not having a clue what a "Good Citizen Award" might entail.

"Just get your bike and ride up to her house. Make sure you're on time." And with that, my mother sent me off to Mrs. Dayock's house to compete for the Edgewater Women's Democratic Club's Good Citizen Award.

Mrs. Dayock was clearly the fanciest lady in Edgewater. Besides being the club's president, she was also the mother of Grace Dayock, an Edgewater girl who, unlike me, had made it onto the cheerleading squad and into the upper ranks of popularity at Leonia High School.

When I got there, Mrs. Dayock showed me into her dining room and introduced me to two other ladies who were sipping tea from the tiniest cups I had ever seen. They held their pinkies high, and I wondered why all three ladies were wearing the same color nail polish. With their bouffant Jackie Kennedy hair and trendy outfits, they looked a lot more sophisticated than my mother. But they didn't look as nice.

Mrs. Dayock offered me the seat opposite them and began, "So, dear, what do *you* think makes a good citizen?"

"A good citizen?" I repeated, fixing my smile to hide my overbite.

"Yes, dear, a good citizen."

"Well . . ." I began, searching my head for the answer to Mrs. Dayock's riddle. "*A nice person?*"

"Yes," she nodded, and prompted, "a nice person *and* . . ."

I thought for a moment about what else might make a good citizen and decided, "Just a nice person, that's all."

"Oh, that's very nice, dear," Mrs. Dayock said as she nodded toward the two other ladies, who nodded back. Mrs. Dayock stood up and gestured toward the door. "We appreciate your coming, dear." Needless to say, my pontification on good citizenry did not win me the thousand dollars.

When I got home from Chicky Dayock's, I assaulted my mother with my tale of woe. "I'm mortified, Mom, just mortified," I sputtered. "Everyone there acted like they were much better than me. And now Mrs. Dayock is going to tell Grace about my stupid answer, Grace will tell the cheerleaders, and the cheerleaders will tell the whole school! I knew I shouldn't have gone. I just knew it!"

Mom threw up her hands. "Enough," she said. "Barbara Ann, just get over yourself! Whether you won or lost isn't even important. What's important is that you had *the right to be there. Period.* Besides, taking yourself *that* seriously will only give you a heart attack."

* * *

Susan crossed her legs and shifted in her chair impatiently. Then it hit me. Susan Cara was simply a rougher version of me. She was hungry, passionate, and desperately trying to fill in the blanks.

"Okay, Susan," I said. "Since your customer is for real, and since you need help in getting access to commercial property owners, let me suggest you talk to Carrie Chiang."

"Who's she?" she snapped.

"Carrie Chiang is the number one broker in this firm," I said, "as well as the number one broker in all of Manhattan. She can get you your appointment with Mr. Trump and with any other commercial developers you need access to. Commercial developers won't give you the time of day, Susan, but they'll give it to Carrie. I'd be happy to walk you over to her desk and introduce you right now if you like."

I knew a woman like her would find the immediacy of my offer appealing and she followed me through the sales area over to Carrie's section. Every salesperson turned, their eyes following her red plaid Chanel suit as her hips swayed side to side in the unmistakable age-old message that screamed, "Come and get it!"

Carrie's office was a frenzy of activity. Like a taxi dispatcher, she was working three phones at once while two assistants shuffled files. We watched and waited for a break. When Carrie finally looked up she said, "Hi, Baa-bwa, what you got?"

"Susan," I answered, "and she wants to meet with Donald Trump. Susan has a big investor from Hong Kong that is interested in the Plaza Hotel."

"Who your investor?" Carrie asked point-blank.

"Polylinks Corporation," Susan answered.

"Daniel Yiu or Jefferson Wu?" Carrie shot back.

Susan was startled. "Both," she answered slowly, squinting her eyes and trying to size Carrie up.

Carrie pushed a chair at Susan and commanded, "Sit down!"

*   *   *

That's how the partnership began. Susan Cara, from Queens, representing Polylinks Corporation from Hong Kong, and Carrie Chiang, from Hong Kong, representing Donald Trump from New York. And both salespeople representing The Corcoran Group.

January 1994. The Plaza Hotel.

Susan, Carrie, and I stood outside the Plaza Hotel waiting for Donald Trump. I was six months pregnant and feeling a little too bloated to be standing in high heels hustling a deal. A swarm of Plaza employees buzzed about on high alert, making all the necessary preparations. In the midst of all the pomp and circumstance, I felt a bit like a pauper about to witness the king's arrival at the palace gates.

At exactly 8:30 A.M., The Donald's black limousine arrived at the red-carpeted Plaza steps. A full squad of uniformed doormen opened the Plaza's brass-plated doors, and they tripped over themselves trying to say hello to Mr. Trump. "Good morning, Mr. Trump! Good morning, Mr. Trump! Mr. Trump! Good morning, sir!" they all chorused.

"Dahnul!" Carrie shouted down, her face flushed with all the excitement. "Hello, Dahnul!" She reached for Donald's hand and pointed to me. "You know Baa-bwa. And this is Susan."

"Good morning, Carrie, Susan," The Donald clipped, giving Susan the once-over. He nodded at her approvingly. "Barbara," he said, hardly looking my way. Without another word, Donald strutted into the Plaza, entourage, including us, in tow.

We were seated at The Donald's corner table in the Edwardian Room, overlooking Central Park South and Fifth Avenue. Donald, his financial guy, and the three of us all awaiting Susan's clients.

A dozen waiters fluttered around Donald, attending to his whims. Carrie pulled out her files and slammed them on the table. "I go over all your numbers, Dahnul," Carrie said directly, "and I don't see numbers on the bank. Where your numbers, Dahnul?"

Donald Trump knew Carrie well. Carrie had single-handedly sold fifty-three condos in Mr. Trump's financially troubled condominium on Sixty-ninth Street in less than a year. She had sold them two at a time, despite the fact that the condominium market had stumbled and all the other new condominium developments weren't selling. Donald was so appreciative he arranged a private dinner at the Plaza Hotel to honor Carrie for her heroic rescue. He presented her with a cake and fifty-three candles, each candle representing an apartment she had sold. Exhilarated by all the attention, Carrie blew them out with one big breath. "In three months, Dahnul," she proclaimed, "I sell fifty-three more!" And Carrie did.

Carrie and Donald continued discussing the numbers, Carrie waving her arms all the while to emphasize her points.

"*Psssst!*" Susan leaned into me and whispered. "*Don't forget the commission agreement.*"

"*What* commission agreement?" I asked.

"Our commission agreement. We don't have one."

"What do you mean we don't have a commission agreement?" I huffed in disbelief. "*Why not?*" Susan fluttered her eyelashes and let out a little-girl giggle.

"Excuse me, Donald," I interrupted. "We need to have a commission agreement."

"Don't worry about it," he answered. "We all know each other here." And he continued to talk to Carrie.

"No, Dahnul!" Carrie said, signaling "stop" with her open hand. "Our commission three percent! Three percent, Dahnul! If Polylink buy Plaza, if Polylink buy condos, if Polylink buy other Dahnul property, *you-pay-me-three-percent*! It commercial commission, Dahnul, *commercial commission three percent*. A good deal, Dahnul," she said, and waited.

"Okay, okay, Carrie, no problem," he said, and looked back down at the financial papers Carrie had brought.

I reached over and pulled the paper doily from underneath the silver sugar tray. I smoothed it out, took a pen, and wrote what I remembered to be the essential elements of a legal contract. It read: "January 11, 1994. I, Donald Trump, promise to pay The Corcoran Group, and I, Barbara Corcoran, promise to accept a three percent (3%) commission for the sale of any currently owned Donald Trump properties sold to Polylinks and/or their affiliates."

I signed my name at the bottom of the doily and drew a line for Donald Trump's signature.

"Donald," I interrupted again, "just to make sure there's no misunderstanding about the commission, I wrote down exactly what we just agreed on." I handed it to him. "Could you please sign right here next to where I signed my name?" I pointed to his name.

Donald took a quick look. "Of course I will," he said and signed his name with a thick black pen and handed me the doily.

I put the doily in my purse and checked my watch; it was 8:47. Messrs. Yiu and Wu were already seventeen minutes late. "Well, Susan?" I said quietly, "Where are they?" When she answered by giggling nervously, I wanted to rip her long legs off her fabulous body.

Donald looked around the room. "Where are the Chinese?" he demanded. "Are they coming or not?"

"Excuse me, Mr. Trump," Susan apologized coyly, pushing a strand of hair away from her face. "I think they may have gone to Trump Tower by mistake. I'll go over and get them."

Ten minutes later, Susan returned with no Wu and no Yiu. She was panting from her two-block sprint and explained that her clients were nowhere to be found. By 9:15, Mr. Trump decided he had waited long enough, but just as he got up to leave, two Chinese men in identical dark blue suits walked into the Edwardian Room.

"Oh, Mr. Yiu! Mr. Wu!" Susan called, swaying her way over. "Come, Mr. Yiu, Mr. Wu. I'd like you to meet Mr. Trump." The Donald stood up, his six-foot-two frame towering over the two men.

"Really nice of you guys to come in and see me," he said, offering his hand. The Asians looked pleased to meet such a New York celebrity.

"And this is Carrie Chiang," Susan continued, "Mr. Trump's broker."

Carrie Chiang stood up and spoke in rapid Mandarin Chinese.

"*Hen rong xing ren shi ni. Xi wang ni ci xing shun li.*"

"*Hen shun li, chen xiao jie,*" Mr. Yiu responded.

"*Wo zhe li lu xing hen shun li.*" Mr. Wu nodded and agreed.

Susan looked unnerved as she lost control of her customer. She escorted them away from Carrie and over to my side of the table, "And this is Barbara Corcoran, Mr. Yiu and Mr. Wu, the president of my company."

"It's a pleasure to meet you," I said, shaking their hands and smiling. Everyone took a seat.

Carrie began her lengthy presentation on the Plaza Hotel. The Chinese men listened intently, punctuating each of her points with nods and questioning her numbers as she went. Carrie talked right, left, and in between, never losing sight of where she was going. She pulled papers, pointed to charts, and worked her calculator. When it came to numbers, Carrie could find a needle in a haystack.

Donald sat quietly, looking distracted, as though he were already involved in some other agenda. And then he made his move. "I've got a strong gut feeling that the Plaza is not the right deal for you. I keep thinking that my Riverside South project might be more what you guys are looking for. It's a really big deal, a *really* big deal! It's going to be the largest commercial and residential project to ever hit Manhattan! Fourteen city blocks right on the Hudson River! Sixteen buildings, six thousand apartments, two million square feet of commercial space, and, would you believe it, underground parking for thirty-five hundred cars! Ready to build. It took me ten years to get the city's approval on this big deal. And Philip Johnson—you know his name, the famous architect—designed the project." He hesitated. "But, you know, guys, I shouldn't be talking about it."

"Mr. Trump, thank you. But we have no interest in new development deals," Mr. Yiu said. "We buy hotels."

"Okay," Donald said, "I probably shouldn't be talking about it anyway, as we've just about signed a deal with Colony Capital. They have a bunch of Japanese investors that are pretty excited about a three hundred percent return on their investment." Then he stopped. "But since you guys are only interested in hotels, I gotta tell you, the Plaza is the best hotel in New York."

The breakfast ended at 10:00. As Carrie promised to send the Chinese the information they needed, Susan corrected her and said, "*I'll* send that to you, Mr. Yiu and Mr. Wu, by next week at the latest."

March 4, 1994.

I was lying in the white-sheeted bed at Mt. Sinai hospital when the phone rang. After six long years and eight failed in vitro attempts, I was aglow with the miracle that I had actually given birth to a healthy nine-pound, two-ounce boy.

"Baa-bwa," a loud voice squawked on the other end of the phone. "Baa-bwa, it's Carrie. I on the plane, I on the plane and I have Dahnul."

"Oh, that's good, Carrie," I said as I shifted to adjust the bandages from my C-section. Carrie and Susan were on their way to China and were calling again to badger me into getting Donald's attorney on the phone.

"Baa-bwa, you call Dahnul's lawyer now," Carrie instructed. "You get Dahnul's lawyer to send the papers now. Okay?"

"Okay, Carrie," I said. "I'm sorry I haven't gotten to it yet but I've been a little busy. Oh, and by the way, I had a baby."

It took five and a half months, nineteen meetings, two trips to Hong Kong, 2,700 pages of faxed documents, and seventeen attorneys, but on June 30, 1994, the deal closed, and the six wealthiest families in Hong Kong became one of the largest landlords in Manhattan, purchasing the outstanding $310 million debt from the banks for the bargain price of $90 million, plus another $8 million in real estate taxes.

※

MOM'S LESSON #21: You have the right to be there.

※

THE LESSON LEARNED ABOUT INVITING YOURSELF IN

When Susan Cara interviewed for her sales position at The Corcoran Group, she explained how she was married to a man who owned an auto repair shop in Brooklyn and how every day she served the mechanics coffee and doughnuts in the morning, and tea and cookies in the afternoon. Susan succeeded in selling fourteen city blocks in Manhattan to a Chinese conglomerate. Nothing in her background said she had the right to be there, but Susan Cara invited herself in.

Susan was inexperienced. But she was also impatient, didn't listen, knew no boundaries, and was relentless in keeping her eye on the ball. It was partly dumb luck that landed the Chinese investors in Susan's lap, but the fact is that once they landed, she had the gumption to take the ball and run.

Carrie Chiang was a proven dealmaker. She, too, was impatient, didn't listen, knew no boundaries, and was relentless in keeping her eye on the ball. Both of them were smart enough to recognize that each had what the other needed. And together they made the biggest sale in New York's history.

* * *

P.S. To no one's surprise, Carrie Chiang continued to smash her own sales records year after year. But Susan's career proved short lived. Soon after the sale, she divorced the mechanic; she snagged herself a renowned internist and retired to their luxurious new abode in Westchester County.

22

You've Got to Bully
a Bully

June 1994.

As it turns out, I had lost the commission doily a few days after the first breakfast at the Plaza and had been too afraid to tell Carrie and Susan. Our attorney knew, and had used it to bluff Donald into agreeing to sign a new commission agreement, threatening to sue on the basis of a doily that didn't exist.

But Donald had negotiated us down and the final agreement stipulated that our commission would be 2 percent and would be paid out monthly over three years. Each installment was due by the tenth business day of every month. And if a payment was late, the entire commission became immediately due.

The week before the deal closed, I picked up the phone and called *New York* magazine, a gossipy New York weekly always eager to break a sensational story. The business editor told me that they were about to run a cover story that said Donald Trump was finished. He said that although Citicorp had already renegotiated Donald's debt of $993 million, they were about to foreclose on Donald's prestigious Plaza Hotel anyway.

"Well, what I'm about to tell you might just change your story," I said.

On the tenth business day of July, Donald's first check arrived, hand-delivered by his messenger at 4:48 P.M. The messenger was instructed to hand it only to me and have me sign the receipt. I called Esther, Carrie, and Susan and waited for them to arrive before opening the envelope and asked Sylvia to immediately send Donald a large bouquet of flashy flowers from Remy's on Park Avenue. I asked that the florist include a note that read, "Thank you for your check, Donald. We so much appreciate it." And sign it Barbara, Carrie, and Susan.

When everyone arrived at our office, we drank champagne and celebrated the first of what would be our thirty-six equal monthly payments of $55,555.55 each.

August 1994.

I gulped when I saw the caricature of Donald Trump on the cover of *New York* magazine, precariously hanging on to the ledge of a high-rise building. I was standing at a newsstand on the corner of Sixtieth and Madison as I read the bold headline:

TRUMP'S NEAR DEATH EXPERIENCE

By the time I got to the office, Donald had already called once. When he called again, I carefully picked up the phone and said as cheerfully as I could, "Good morning, Donald."

Donald's voice barked into my ear. *"How could you let Carrie and that Susan lady speak to a reporter? Can't you keep your girls in check over there!"*

"Donald," I said, "you know I'm not in control of Carrie, you know how she is. And as for Susan, she's young and inexperienced, and you can't fault her for that. But, personally, I think today's story makes you look great! In fact, I think it makes you look like a miracle worker—" Donald Trump didn't agree with my assessment and abruptly hung up the phone.

When the next check arrived, again by messenger, I signed for it and instructed Sylvia to send an even larger bouquet of flashy flowers. Two hours later, the bouquet arrived back at my office, returned by Mr. Trump's messenger. On the unopened envelope was scribbled, "Return to sender." I got a sick feeling in my stomach that things were about to get worse.

Things got worse. The next day, the summons and complaint arrived, claiming "breach of contract." Donald was suing *us* to cancel the $2 million commission (not yet paid) and to recover damages.

SUPREME COURT OF THE STATE OF NEW YORK
COUNTY OF NEW YORK
---------------- X
DONALD TRUMP,

Plaintiff,

-against-

THE CORCORAN GROUP, INC.,
BARBARA CORCORAN, CARRIE CHIANG
and SUSAN CARA,

Defendants.
_____ X

60 Centre Street
New York, New York
May 20, 1996

BEFORE :HONORABLE IRA GAMMERMAN, JUSTICE

"Let's get a big guy!" Carrie said. "Dahnul not fair! We need a *big* lawyer." Susan agreed with Carrie, but Esther had already met with our regular attorney and, after reviewing the papers, he said he was confident he could win the case. Although I wanted to believe in his confidence, something gnawed at me after everyone left my office.

I opened my drawer, took out the *New York* magazine article, and found the passage that was echoing in my brain. Donald was quoted as saying, "You learn that either you're the toughest, meanest piece of shit in the world or you just crawl into a corner, put your finger in your mouth, and say, 'I want to go home.' "

A chill ran up my spine.

After school. The kitchen table.

My brother Tommy was so upset he couldn't tell my mother what was wrong. "Well, you can't stay in here all day," Mom said. "You should be outside playing with the other boys."

"I don't *want* to," Tommy cried. "I don't want to go outside and see that kid again!"

"And what kid is that?" Mom asked, wiping Tommy's face with a cold washcloth.

"J-Joey B-Bunt," Tommy said. "He says really mean things to me, Mom, and he embarrasses me in front of all the other boys."

John boosted himself up on to the counter and reached for the pinwheels that Mom kept hidden above the stove. "Isn't that the same kid who puts cherry bombs in cats?" John asked.

"He does what?" Mom asked.

"Yeah, that's him, that's the same mean kid," Tommy sniffled. "And that's not all! He's a big bully! I saw him kick Mrs. Gibbon's dog—you know, the little scrawny one with the brown spots."

"Well, Tommy," Mom said, "sooner or later you're going to have to face him, because he's probably not planning to move out of Edgewater."

"Yeah, and I'll go with you, Tom," John offered confidently.

"Well, if he's a bully," Mom said, "you're going to need more than two nice boys to handle him. Let me call Mrs. Higgins and ask if Brendan can go with you."

"We don't need Brendan to come with us, Mom," John said. "I'm big enough."

"Oh, no you're not," Mom insisted. "You've got to bully a bully, and Brendan can do that easier because he's bigger."

That day, Brendan Higgins whipped Joey Bunt's butt and Joey never bothered my brother Tommy again.

I picked up the phone and called Carrie. "Carrie," I said, "you're right. We need to find ourselves a great litigator to fight Mr. Trump."

1996. Supreme Court of the State of New York.

The moment Richard Seltzer walked into the courtroom, I knew we weren't going to be pushed around. Richard was just the right guy, tough enough and smart enough to bully a bully. I had to remind myself that the ball of fire burning up the courtroom was the same quiet attorney who had spent hours meticulously reviewing every possible question that we might be asked.

Donald Trump's claim was that, as his agent, we had breached our fiduciary responsibility by disclosing confidential information in the *New York* magazine article. Our defense was that everything Carrie and Susan said in the article was *not* confidential, because Donald had already bragged the same details to dozens of other reporters before the *New York* magazine story ever came out.

Donald looked startled when Richard Seltzer pulled out his stack of four-color, five-foot charts with blown-up quotes of what Donald had said, when, and to whom. He had prepared separate boards quoting Donald spilling the beans to the *Wall Street Journal* on

June 8, to the *South China Morning Post* on June 10, to the *New York Observer* on June 13, and to *Crain's New York Business* on June 20. "Are these not your quotes, Mr. Trump?!?" Richard demanded in a booming voice as he cross-examined Donald on the stand.

In rendering his decision, Judge Ira Gammerman said, "Of all the witnesses, my view is that Miss Corcoran's recollection is the most reliable. I tell you that. . . . And I find as a matter of fact that there was no fraudulent inducement. We have a *bruised ego*, is what this case is all about. And I'm telling you, I find, as a matter of fact, that those are the only damages in this case."

We won the suit and collected the rest of our $2 million commission.

✳

MOM'S LESSON #22: You've got to bully a bully.

✳

THE LESSON LEARNED ABOUT BEATING BULLIES

We were paid our rightful commission because we spent the money to hire the right attorney. Despite my best efforts to convince The Donald to settle our differences outside the courtroom, in the end we had to hire a bully beater so the bully didn't win.

Before finding Richard Seltzer at Kaye Scholer LLP, we interviewed the best litigators at other top New York law firms but none of them measured up to Richard Seltzer. Here are three tips for choosing the right attorney:

1. **It's not about knowing the law.**

   All attorneys know the law. It's not how well they know the law that counts, it's how well they play the law to their advantage.

2. **The right attorney has one unique selling proposition.**

   All litigators can rattle off a half-dozen ideas on how to defeat the opposing side. The right attorney presents and believes 100 percent in one good idea.

3. **Winning in court has more to do with sales and packaging than it has to do with law.**

   Good litigators are great communicators and exceptional salespeople. Careful preparation and presentation of the facts is more important than the facts themselves.

23

Never Be Ashamed
of Who You Are

December 1997.

"Howard Milstein on the phone," Sylvia announced.

I had never met Mr. Howard Milstein, but rumor had it that the New York billionaire had paid only $12 million to buy my competitor six years earlier. He had bought the Douglas Elliman Real Estate Company at the depth of the real estate recession from a group of investors who had milked the company dry. Twelve million dollars sounded like a ton of money to me, but people in the finance field called it a bargain-basement price.

Under Mr. Milstein's leadership, Douglas Elliman combined the one-two punch of old-money prestige and good-old-boy power. Although his company had a larger market share than we did, The Corcoran Group was gaining fast, and I suspected that Mr. Milstein didn't like that very much.

"Hi, it's Barbara," I chirped as I picked up the phone, wondering why my archrival was calling me.

"Hold for Mr. Milstein," his secretary said, and put me on hold in what I find to be one of the most annoying practices of people in power.

"Good morning, Barbara," a clipped but polite voice said on the other end of the phone. "I'd like to get together and discuss some business."

"Some business?" I asked. "What kind of business?"

"*Our* business," he said. "Let's discuss it over a cocktail, shall we? How about tomorrow?"

"I can't," I said with relief. "I'm leaving with my family for a vacation in Australia tomorrow and will be gone for two weeks."

"Fine, then let's say two weeks from tomorrow," he agreed. "That will be the twenty-fourth. We'll meet at my home. Shall we say four P.M.?"

Before I could say "jet lag," I had agreed to the date.

The twenty-four hours back from Australia seemed a lot longer than the twenty-four hours getting there, and when I landed at JFK airport, I had exactly eighty minutes to find my luggage, hop a cab to Manhattan, change clothes, and present myself at Mr. Milstein's home on Park Avenue.

I got home, dropped my luggage, threw on a suit, and headed out. I stopped at a Korean fruit stand on Lexington Avenue and quickly paid for a bunch of daisies. "No need to wrap," I said, and rushed over to Park Avenue and Seventy-eighth Street. When I arrived at Mr. Milstein's building, a uniformed doorman with lots of gold braiding announced my arrival.

"Miss Corcoran for Mr. Milstein," he said into the front-door phone. He motioned me toward another man in gold braid, who ushered me into a brass-gated elevator. When the elevator doors opened, I didn't have to guess which door was Mr. Milstein's. There was only one. The door was made of gleaming mahogany, and standing at attention holding it open was a man in a long-tailed coat. He looked as if he was dressed for a wedding.

"Goooood afternoooon!" he said, finishing his *o*'s and bowing his head as if to collect a thought he'd lost. "Mr. Milstein is expecting you, m'daahm. Please follow me."

He turned on his heel like a palace guard, and, feeling rather awkward, I followed behind. The huge entrance gallery was bigger than our house in Edgewater and it had some serious museum-type paintings hanging on the walls. There were lots of tables decorated with the largest flower arrangements I'd ever seen. "Please wait here, m'daahm," he instructed as we got to the middle of the runway. "I'll tell Mr. Milstein you've arrived." I tucked my Korean deli daisies behind my back and was thinking about stashing them under one of the big tables when Mr. Milstein suddenly appeared.

"So nice of you to come, Barbara!" he welcomed, while eagerly shaking my hand. "Perhaps we'll sit in the den, James," he said. James nodded, turned on his heel, and walked back in the direction we had just come. I followed along again, with Mr. Milstein bringing up the rear.

Mr. Milstein looked surprised to find Mrs. Milstein sitting in the den. He politely introduced me, and she politely helloed me back, and I decided it was as good a time as any to unload my three-dollar daisies.

I pulled the daisies from behind my back and felt like Timmy Tom when he handed my mother the gladiolus he'd yanked from our yard. "These are for you, Mrs. Milstein," I said. Mrs. Milstein hesitated, and then took them, ignoring the rubber band at the bottom. "Why, thank you," she said softly, "how sweet."

"You're welcome," I said, smiling, but somehow felt I had done something wrong.

"Let us try the library then, shall we?" Mr. Milstein pleasantly decided, and again we trotted off into the gallery, led by James. "Good-bye," I quickly said to Mrs. Milstein and the daisies.

The trip down the Milstein runway was beginning to feel like the flight back from Australia, and when we finally arrived at the library, James ceremoniously opened the heavy paneled doors to a huge room filled with books, chairs, and tables and lamps all around. James stepped to the side, folding his arms behind his back.

"What will you have to drink, Barbara?" Mr. Milstein asked as he motioned to a brown leather club chair.

"White wine, please," I said, settling in.

"And what kind would you prefer?" he asked with a tight smile.

"White, thank you," I replied.

James walked out, quietly closing the doors behind him. I sat straight in my chair, smiling, and trying to figure out why I was there.

"The Corcoran Group seems to be progressing quite nicely," Mr. Milstein offered.

"Why, thank you, Mr. Milstein," I said, scanning the plaques, trophies, and diplomas that surrounded us. "It's very nice of you to say that, Mr. Milstein, and I really appreciate hearing it."

"Barbara, please call me Howard."

"Okay, then, Howard, please call me Barbara."

I decided to keep quiet for a while because I didn't know what to talk about, and although Mr. Milstein—I mean, Howard—was talking to me as though I was his new best friend, I kept thinking of him as my competitor, and didn't think those two things usually came together. James walked back in, handed each of us our drink, set down some small plates and napkins, and left.

"I really do admire how far you've come with your company, Barbara," Mr. Milstein continued. "You strike me as a very smart businesswoman."

"Thank you, Howard," I said, feeling more uncomfortable than smart. "But I'm really not smart at all, I just work really hard." I took a chug of my wine.

"Well, I'm sure you're smart enough to recognize a good business idea when you hear one. I think we could have great synergism if we were to work together."

"Sinner-jizzum," I repeated slowly. "I'm embarrassed to admit that I don't know what that word means." I realized I was way out of my league, and probably shouldn't have come.

Mr. Milstein closed his hands with his forefingers raised in a V, leaned way back in his chair, and expounded, "Well, Barbara, then let me take a moment to explain it to you. Synergism is a business term I learned at Harvard. It simply means joining two strong companies to create a stronger one that's able to do more business. It's really quite simple, like one plus one equals three."

"I think I get it," I said. "Yes, one plus one equals three! You're really a wonderful teacher and you obviously know a lot about business, Mr. Milstein! Now, what two companies were you thinking about putting together?"

"What? Well, mine and yours, of course!"

The mahogany doors opened and James wheeled in a large silver cart. He lifted a tray, genuflected in front of me, and said, "*Ooorrr durrrr*ve?"

I looked down at the food in front of me. I was ferociously hungry and beginning to feel the jet lag and wine settling in. The food on the tray didn't look like anything I'd seen before. It looked a little bit like mini-burritos, but not exactly, because it had pink stuff inside. There were also little black things on top that looked like chocolate sprinkles. But I leaned in for a closer look and, though I had never tried caviar before, I realized by its wetness that that's probably what it was.

"M'daahm?" James offered, waiting in his bent position.

I decided to go for it because I thought it would be rude not to, and I was also really hungry. "Oh, thank you," I said.

Using my hand like the metal claw at the Palisades Amusement Park crane game, I reached down for the "burrito." I tried to get a good hold on it, but it was wetter than I thought and both the pink stuff and the caviar sprinkles kept sliding around. Finally, I grabbed it and popped the sucker into my mouth. The burrito filled every bit of my mouth, and I could hardly chew.

"Will that be . . . all, m'daahm?" James asked without moving, his eyes wide, as if he were giving me a signal to take more.

I shook my head no and answered, "Hwumm hwmum," which was my stuffed-mouth version of "Thank you, James, that will be all."

James moved over to Mr. Milstein and offered him the tray. Mr. Milstein took a small silver fork and knife and a little plate from the table between us. He lifted a burrito and gracefully placed it on his plate. As I continued trying to chew, Mr. Milstein cut off a small piece, nudged it onto his fork, and tipped it into his mouth. He nodded at James and said, "*Mmmm*, perfect!"

Oh, God, I thought, gumming at my mouthful of mush, *so that's what the little knife and fork were for!*

Girl Scouts. The Fort Lee Pizzeria.

The first time I ever had pizza was with Miss Griffin and seven Girl Scouts. Miss Griffin, our eighth-grade teacher, was the only Holy Rosary School teacher who wasn't a nun. She had taken us to see *To Kill a Mockingbird* at the Fort Lee Movie Theater, and afterward, we went to the Fort Lee Pizzeria to have pizza.

When our pizza came, we all lifted a slice onto our paper plates and waited for it to cool. I followed Grace Dayock's lead on how to eat it. Grace raised the pizza to her mouth and chomped down. I raised my pizza to my mouth and chomped down too. But my teeth couldn't cut the cheese. My overbite wouldn't allow it.

I kept the pizza against my lips and looked around the table. The other Girl Scouts were well into their slices and hadn't noticed the pizza still stuck in my mouth. I grated my teeth back and forth, but the cheese just shifted along with my teeth. I opened my mouth to let go of the pizza, folded the dented tip back onto the slice, and quietly put the pizza back on my plate.

When I got home, Mom had just finished her bath. "What's for dinner, Mom?" I said through the bathroom door.

"Nothing," she answered, "dinner was at six. Didn't you eat dinner with the Girl Scouts and Miss Griffin?"

"Nope."

"Well, why not?" Mom asked, as she came out of the bathroom.

"My overbite wouldn't let me eat the pizza."

"That's pretty funny," she laughed. "So, why didn't you ask for a plate of spaghetti or something? Or just a knife and fork?"

"I couldn't," I said. "I was too embarrassed."

"Embarrassed? Why would you be embarrassed?"

"I didn't want anyone to see my buckteeth."

"Ha! That's ridiculous!" Mom huffed. "I'm sure the Girl Scouts have seen your buckteeth before. Besides, Barbara Ann, you have a beautiful smile, and you should never be ashamed of who you are. Now, why don't you go over to the refrigerator and find yourself something to eat."

Mr. Milstein spoke slowly. "Let me explain to you some of the synergisms we might enjoy together," he said. "Take advertising, for example. We would have a lot more buying clout and be able to negotiate substantial discounts if we were together."

"*Hmmmm,*" I answered, my eyes watering as I swallowed the tail end of the fishy mush.

"And we could cut the expenses of our back-office operations in half," he suggested, "possibly in thirds. We could also combine our individual offices and keep only the best salespeople. I'm sure you're carrying a lot of deadwood, like we are, and together we could eliminate it.

"And you could run both businesses!" he enthused. "And you'd be in charge of many more people than you are now."

James came back in and lowered his tray to offer me another burrito. "M'daahm?" he asked again. I stared down at the tray of food I didn't want, but, not wanting to offend my host, and not wanting to offend James for offering it, I decided I'd better take another.

I looked at the little knife and fork on the table next to my chair. With them I could eat as delicately as Mr. Milstein. But thinking about my mother, I decided I didn't want to.

"Oh, thank you," I said.

I lifted my hand and craned it over a burrito. Grabbing it dead center, I popped it into my mouth. *"Mmmm."* I smiled.

Mr. Milstein talked on and on about synergies, market shares, diminishing returns, and a lot of other things that I wasn't educated enough to know about, had always heard about, and didn't really care about. Then he began his grand finale.

"Barbara, together our companies would have the majority control of the Manhattan real estate market," he said. "And our combined companies could be sold for a lot more money than if we sold them separately."

I looked at Mr. Milstein and tried to picture him as my partner. Or would he be my employer? I wasn't sure. Maybe he just wanted to buy me wholesale and sell me retail. I didn't know.

"Well then, what do you think?" he asked confidently as he inched toward me in his leather chair.

"Would you like a political answer or an honest one?" I asked.

"An honest answer, of course," he said.

"No," I said. And with that, I thanked Mr. Milstein for the delicious food and the wonderful education and bade him good-bye.

✷

MOM'S LESSON #23: Never be ashamed of who you are.

✷

THE LESSON LEARNED
ABOUT BEING YOURSELF

Sometimes people fail to realize that their personal points of difference are, in fact, often their best advantages, and that everyone likes and responds best to people who are comfortable with themselves.

Everyone recognizes someone who's genuine, especially in business, where group pressure often imposes the status quo of expected business behavior. I was never afraid to be different and got to where I was by being myself. Although I wasn't fancy and didn't have a business degree, I did have common sense and the ability to laugh at myself.

Mr. Milstein's offer turned out to be the first in a long line of similar propositions. But none of my suitors ever asked what my dreams and aspirations were *before* they started their sales pitch. If they had, they would have discovered that my personal goals had nothing to do with money, status, or power.

But my visit with Mr. Milstein got me thinking, and for the first time, I realized I had a business actually worth something! I decided to size up where I had been, where I was now, and, most important, where I wanted to go.

I realized that my dream of being the "Queen of New York Real Estate" had come true. I had taken the company from Ray Simone's $1,000 investment and the 1 BR + DEN ad to what was about to become the number one firm in the New York market. I had climbed my mountain and achieved everything I had set out to do, and had proven to myself that I could "succeed without him."

Thanks to the fabulous market of the nineties, The Corcoran Group was hugely profitable and had ended the year with more than $2 billion in sales. Our salespeople and employees were known as the best in the business. We had twelve beautifully designed offices equipped with the most advanced technology, and it was *all* paid for. In short, The Corcoran Group was in mint condition.

But I had seen bad times, too, and considered myself lucky to have made it through. With our overhead now more than a million dollars a month, liquidating my personal assets wouldn't be enough to carry the business through another downturn. I knew we needed deeper pockets.

I thought about taking on a financial partner as a minority shareholder, but knew that in bad times the partner with the most money often wrestles away majority control. I realized I was much too independent for that.

What I treasured most about building the business was working with all our great people and running the company hand-in-hand like a family. But now there were so many people at the company, I no longer knew each person's name, and that bothered me.

Most importantly, I was now the mother of a little boy, and my heart was torn between my family at home and my family at work. I felt guilty when I wasn't with my son and guilty when I wasn't with my business. My pursuit of the elusive balance that every working mom chases was proving impossible.

I came to the realization that my business was all grown up, and ready to leave mom and go out on its own. I soon found someone who not only offered me the right price, but also offered me enough freedom and enough latitude to continue making The Corcoran Group the best in the business.

Besides, I had been "Barbara Corcoran, the real estate lady" for so long, I started thinking it might be nice to see what it was like to be just Barbara Corcoran.

24
The Joy Is in the
Getting There

September 2001.

As we turned the corner onto Madison Avenue, I was cherishing
the fact that my seven-year-old son was still willing to walk beside
me and hold my hand. But, as usual, he dropped it at the first sight-
ing of the bigger boys standing in front of his school and gave me his
quick-while-nobody's-looking sideways hug and darted inside. As
the door closed behind him, I thought, *My God, how fast it's going*,
and mourned the end of another day walking my little boy to school.

I stopped by our new real estate office on the corner of Madison
Avenue and picked up the packet of newspaper clippings my assistant, Sheryl, had left for me to read. I tucked the envelope under my
arm, crossed over to the Korean deli, and picked out my weekly
bunch of six-dollar flowers. As I got to the cashier, I remembered I
didn't have any cash. I apologized, put the flowers back, and made a
beeline to the ATM at the Citibank across the street.

All the machines were taken, and I stood in line behind a woman whose gray-and-white hair was styled just like her Yorkie's. When it was my turn, I stepped up to the machine on the far left side, put in my bankcard, entered my security code, tapped "Fast Cash," then "$200." I heard the familiar tat-a-tat-a-tat, tat-a-tat-a-tat, as the machine counted out the money, and was relieved to hear the *errrrrrk* as the stack of twenties slid out the front. I put the cash in my Filofax and took the receipt.

On my way to the garbage can by the front window, I took a quick look at the receipt before tossing it in. My arm screeched to a halt. I stared at the receipt in utter disbelief and moved it closer, squinting my eyes to make sure I wasn't imagining things. I turned my head left and then right like an owl, looking to see if anyone was watching. No one was. The Yorkie lady passed me and smiled. Moving closer to the window, I tilted the receipt toward the light to take another look.

Date	Time	Location		Card Number
Sep 25, 2001	08:37	000062		Ending in 036
1275 Madison, NY, NY				
Transaction			Amount	Description
GOT CASH			$200.00	FROM CHECKING
BALANCES				
On deposit			$46,732,917.32	CHECKING
Available now			$46,732,917.32	
citibank®				

Yes, the balance really did read $46,732,917.32! I was *sure* of it. *My God*, I thought, *I've got to show this to someone!* The six people standing at the teller machines had their backs to me, and suddenly the thought of showing any of them my receipt seemed ridiculous. But I just couldn't go home. I needed to do *something* to celebrate.

I carefully folded the blue-and-white receipt in half, tucked it into my bra, and walked over to the diner next door. I picked a seat at the empty table by the window and quickly straightened out the sugar container, ketchup bottle, and salt and pepper shakers, before the waitress came over.

"What can I get you, honey?" she asked.

What the heck, I thought, *I'll go whole hog today. After all, this isn't just any old day!* "I'll have eggs Benedict, a large glass of orange juice, and coffee, please," I said. The waitress was wearing a rhinestone heart pinned to her white collar, and I added, "That's really a lovely pin you have there."

"Oh, thank you," she said, seeming grateful that I had noticed. "It was my mother's."

When my eggs arrived, I took out the Citibank receipt from my bra, smoothed out the crease, and leaned it against the sugar dispenser. I took a sip of hot coffee and wondered if Esther had visited *her* bank yet. I laughed at the thought of Esther quickly tucking her bank receipt into her pocketbook and snapping it shut. I remembered the chart I'd drawn the day I talked Esther into becoming my partner, and the wild projections of how far we would go. Things had turned out even bigger than we had dared to imagine.

I thought about all the incredible adventures we had had building the business, and how lucky I was to have been given the freedom to create a world just as I dreamed it could be. I thought about the people who had stood by me through thick and thin, and how everyone at The Corcoran Group had built great lives for themselves. And I felt the immense satisfaction of a job well done.

The boring man at the next table was telling his sister all the news she had missed while she was away on a trip of some kind. He yakked on and on about the bad economy, Republican politics, and the city's terrible school system. When they were finished, the man paid the bill, turned to his sister, and said, "Oh, and did you hear Barbara Corcoran sold her business for mega-millions?" He didn't wait for a response before adding, "Must be nice to have all that money in the bank."

Yes, I guess it is, I reflected, but the *real* joy has been in getting here.

I opened the packet of newspaper articles and read through the pile of clippings.

The New York Times
TUESDAY, SEPTEMBER 25, 2001

Corcoran Sells Realty Firm She Founded

Cashing Out After Years Of Rising Housing Prices

By ANDREW ROSS SORKIN

Barbara Corcoran, the powerhouse Manhattan real estate broker, agreed yesterday to sell the firm she founded, the Corcoran Group.

. . . .

NEW YORK POST
LATE CITY FINAL
September 25, 2001

It's official: Corcoran to Cendant

By BRADEN KEIL

Following an emotionally charged company meeting last Friday, Barbara Corcoran sent a memo to company employees announcing the sale of the Corcoran Group.

NEW YORK BUSINESS®

October 1–7, 2001

Corcoran's home run

. . . Although terms of the transaction weren't disclosed, people close to the deal say it was priced at $70 million.

. . . .

OUR TOWN

Queen of NY Real Estate

If you're looking for new digs in New York, and dwell in one of the loftier tax brackets, chances are you've heard of Barbara Corcoran. Even if you're having trouble making the rent on that studio in Astoria, you know her face. She's the shorthaired blonde sporting an incandescent smile in that commercial with the catchy song and fabulous apartments. In her 28 years as head of the Corcoran Group, she has reached the pinnacle of the toughest real estate market this side of Tokyo.

WOMEN'S BUSINESS

October 2001

After Merger, Corcoran Group Remains Fully Intact

...and that equates to a tremendous increase in business since 1973, when Corcoran began selling real estate from her Manhattan apartment on a $1000-loan from her former boyfriend. He footed the cash for her new venture on the condition that he would own a controlling interest.

Eventually, Corcoran dissolved the partnership. From that moment on, she was bound and determined to make it in the real estate business on her own. By all accounts, she has achieved her goal.

Corcoran has been dubbed the "most sought after broker in the city," according to CNN, and is known as the broker to Hollywood celebrities and wealthy individuals.

Exactly how did the Edgewater, NJ native become one of the most powerful figures in New York City real estate?

"Exactly how?" I repeated the article's question. "My mother," I answered.

I slid a twenty under the saucer and headed back to my apartment. I had an important call to make.

"Hello, Mom. It's Barb. Can you get Dad on the line?"

"Eddie, pick up the phone! It's Barb."

"Hi, Mom. Hi, Dad. You'll never believe what happened at the bank today," I began. Then I told my parents about waiting in line for the teller machine, getting my usual $200 cash, and how I couldn't believe my eyes when I looked down at the receipt. "I'm telling you, Mom, I just couldn't believe it! I thought I was seeing things!"

"Well, what did you do?" Mom asked excitedly.

"I did just what you would have done. I went and had some breakfast and sat there staring at the receipt."

"What'd you eat?" Dad asked.

"Eat? Oh, eggs Benedict."

"Eggs, what?"

"Never mind, Eddie," Mom interrupted. "Go on! Go on!"

"So, I sat at the diner, and I thought about how it's true what you've always said, Mom, the joy really *is* in the getting there."

"Well, that's because it is," she agreed. "But just think about what you've done, Barbara! It really is unbelievable, isn't it?

"Yeah, I guess it really is."

And then I said what I'd wanted to say for a very long time. "In the end, Mom, it all comes down to this. All my life, you never told me I couldn't. You only told me I could."

THE END

Bonus Manual

WHAT MOM DIDN'T TEACH ME BUT EXPERIENCE DID

INTRODUCTION

Every great entrepreneur is a great salesperson, and I have three personal beliefs about selling *anything*.

1. **People want to do business with someone they like.**

   Don't be misled into thinking that sales is all about the product. It's not. It's all about the people. It's as simple as this, if people like you, they're going to want to do business with you. And if they don't, you're going to have an almost insurmountable obstacle to overcome.

2. **Selling is nothing more than playing *up* the good and playing *down* the bad.**

   If you know how to do it naturally, you're a born salesperson, and if not, it can be learned.

3. **Always remember who's in charge of the market you're selling in.**

   In a buyer's market, the *buyer is always right*. In a seller's market, the *seller is always right*. But in an in-between market, *nobody's right*! And it's in this market that salespeople make the most money, because that's when there's the most uncertainty and the most scope for negotiating win-win deals.

TRAITS   RULES   PLANNING   PHONING   CUSTOMERS   PRESENTING   CLOSING   SLUMPS

PART 1

The Most Amazing, Extraordinary, and Distinguishing Characteristics of Great Salespeople

1. Great salespeople fail well.

Great salespeople get knocked down like everyone else, but take a lot less time getting up. In fact, the lowest rate of suicide is among commission salespeople because in the course of a normal day, they field so many rejections that even when life strikes them some extra-difficult blows, they bounce back out of habit.

2. Great salespeople are passionate!

Great salespeople have an attitude of "I'll either succeed, or I'll die trying!" You can't fake passion. There is nothing harder to resist than a passionate salesperson.

3. Great salespeople make lousy employees.

Great salespeople are creative, maverick personalities who put a lot of effort into their jobs, and do them well, provided no one tells them how to do it.

4. Great salespeople have split personalities.

Great salespeople are sometimes miserable to live with, but on the outside they're always masterful charmers.

5. **Great salespeople listen between the lines.**

With great salespeople, there's no such thing as idle conversation, even a pleasant conversation is really an interview.

6. **Great salespeople can talk a dog off a meat wagon.**

Spend more than five minutes with a great salesperson, and you'll walk away swearing their idea was your idea.

7. **Great salespeople know when to cut bait.**

Great salespeople recognize when they're *not* in the right place, at the right time, or with the right customer. They have the confidence to walk away.

8. **Great salespeople believe their success is only temporary.**

Every great salesperson ends each year convinced they will never have another good year. They have a hard time believing they can improve on or even repeat yesterday's sales, until of course they do, and then the whole cycle of fear and accomplishment begins again.

PART 2
The Ten Reliable, Verifiable, Absolutely Undeniable Rules for Getting Ahead

1. **Get outside.**

   Selling is a face-to-face business.

2. **Dress the part.**

   People *do* judge a book by its cover!

3. **Spend your time wisely.**

   There are really only two hundred and twenty selling days in a year. The difference between a mediocre and a phenomenal performance is how well you use your time.

4. **Always tell the truth, *always*.**

   Never fudge anything; it will always come back and bite you.

5. **Do your homework.**

   Knowledge is the best shortcut to earning a customer's trust.

6. **Walk in their shoes.**

   "I understand" are the two most powerful words in the sales business.

7. **Build your referral base just like a pyramid.**

   The wider the base, the higher the peak.

8. **Everybody wants what everybody wants. And nobody wants what nobody wants.**

   It's the basic psychology of sales.

9. **Make a road map.**

   Without a clear plan, you won't know where you're going, and you'll have little chance of getting there.

10. **Go out and play.**

    All the good ideas are on the outside. Besides, nothing really fun ever happens at the office.

PART 3
How to Make a
Business Plan that Works

I've never met a great salesperson who didn't have a plan. With a good plan, you'll have a long-term view of where you want to go and a specific way to get there.

A good business plan should match the way you think. There's a left-brain and a right-brain approach:

"It's the Money, Honey!" (The left-brain logical approach)

The first thing you do is decide how much money you want to make, and then work your plan backwards.

Let's say you want to earn $100,000 a year. Figure out what your average commission is likely to be, let's use $6,000. Now, divide your desired earnings by the average commission and the answer is roughly eighteen sales a year, or 1½ sales each month.

Okay, what will you have to do to make 1½ sales a month?

"Paint a Pretty Picture." (The right-brain visual approach)

This plan is for daydreamers. The first thing you do is visualize yourself as an incredibly successful salesperson. Where are you, what do you look like, what are you wearing, and how do you feel? Fill in every detail and play that picture over and over again in your mind. This picture becomes your road map.

Okay, what will you have to do to make every detail of your picture come true?

How to Make Your Map

1. Set aside a day in your calendar.
Set aside *now*.

2. Pick a place away from your desk.
Choose a place where you can't be interrupted. For me, the library has proven to be the best spot.

3. Organize your reference materials.
Bring your calendar, a list of your past sales, your current customers, and your leads. Also bring any business cards you've collected in the course of doing business.

4. Create a contact file.
Now, make a list of your past customers and contacts (whether you've sold them something or not) and put their names and addresses on mailing labels. Send something to them this week and every six months thereafter. *What* you mail is less important than *that* you mail.

5. Make a list of your individual strengths and weaknesses.
Everyone has different skills and talents, and to capitalize on them you'll need to know yours. If you can't figure them out, ask for the opinion of people who know you.

6. Take a good look at your past sales.
Identify where each of your customers actually came from and jot the source next to each name. With a clear picture of your

best sources of business, you'll be in a better position to get more of it.

7. Figure out what your customers have in common.

Salespeople become more successful once they've figured out who they sell best to. You'll probably discover that you sell best to people similar to you.

8. Rate your customers.

Rating your customers is simply deciding who you should spend your time with. Rate them *based on need*. The "A"s are the customers you should call tomorrow at the latest, the "B"s can wait till next week, and the "C"s should be thrown away. Don't be misled by customers with big budgets; they're often the biggest time wasters.

9. Make a "Not to Do List."

Figure out which past efforts amounted to nothing and label them your "Not to Do List." Post the list where you'll see it.

10. Expand on your best sources of business.

With an understanding of your best sources of leads, you can play to your strengths. For example, if most of your leads are from social contacts, spend more time socializing.

11. Find three new ways to get more business.

Design a marketplace report, create a personal newsletter, host a dinner party, produce a seminar, be a guest speaker, advertise your services, take a vacation, etc. Pick three.

12. Hire some help.

If you feel overwhelmed, you need an assistant. And when you calculate how much *you* make by the hour, you won't hesitate to spend the money. An assistant can answer calls, schedule appointments, fax, file, e-mail, research, create sales presentations, and keep on top of your inventory. Picture your life with less responsibility for the minutiae.

13. Set aside your next planning day now.
Schedule a day six months out.

PART 4
How to Pick Up, Speak Up, and Hang Up the Phone

Salespeople spend at least a third of their time on the phone, more than they do working with customers and showing product. And with the advent of cell phones and e-mail, even more of the sale transaction is now done by phone. I've found that customers don't really want to talk to a salesperson who "sounds professional." They'd rather speak with someone who's friendly, enthusiastic, and informed.

Checklist to get more out of your phone time

❏ *To speak forcefully, stand up.*
Standing up gives you power, and since the guy on the other end is sitting down, you immediately take the upper hand.

❏ *Buy a mirror.*
Put it near your phone and smile into it. Smiling on the phone is heard in your voice.

❏ *Tape-record your voice.*
Listen to yourself while on the phone with a customer. The changes you'll make will increase your appointments by a third.

❏ *Use your answering machine as you would a secretary.*
Be time-specific as to *when* you'll return. No one would ever instruct a secretary, "If anyone calls, tell them I'll call them back as soon as I can."

❏ *Never answer a sales call without a backup list in hand.*
In real estate, customers rarely buy the house they call on, so the salesperson needs to have other properties to offer in order to win the customer's confidence and get the appointment.

❏ *Repeat back the attributes that got the customer to call in the first place.*
When customers call in response to a specific advertisement, they like what they saw, so sell the same attributes back. In real estate, a customer calling about a newspaper ad is looking for a reason to end the call and get on to the next one.

❏ *The objective of every phone call is to get the appointment.*
Get the appointment and *then* worry about finding the right product to show.

❏ *Never confess that you don't know something.*
Instead say, "I'll find out and get right back to you."

❏ *Put in a separate work line or cell phone at home.*
If you must take calls at home, a designated line will allow you to answer knowing it's a customer. It also puts a lot less stress on your family.

❏ *Push the hang-up button in midsentence.*
If you can't get off the phone with a long-winded-going-nowhere caller, press the disconnect button while *you're* talking. You'll end the conversation and the caller will never suspect that you hung up on yourself.

PHONING

PART 5
How to Educate, Motivate, and Satiate the Customer!

Buyers come in different flavors. There are the romantics, the pioneers, the bargain hunters, and the status seekers. If you want to be successful in sales, you'd better be able to figure out what kind of buyer you have. You can do that by finding out what motivates him.

Checklist for working with customers

❏ *Always ask, "When do you want it?"*
The answer will determine more than anything else whether or not you'll be able to make the sale. The best answer: "I need it tomorrow." The worst answer: "Oh, anytime . . ."

❏ *Control the customer's time.*
When you control the customer's time, you control the customer.

❏ *Make every customer feel that he or she is your most important customer.*
Customers really *don't* want to hear about your other customers. They should feel they're your only one.

❏ *Don't take a customer's "requirements" too seriously.*
Everyone wants more than they can afford. Validate the customer by playing back exactly what he said and thinks he wants. Then show him what he really wants, but was unable to articulate.

❑ *When customers aren't realistic,* **tell them.**
Don't be afraid to tell a customer that he's not going to find what he wants. You'll both save a lot of time.

❑ *Show high!*
A buyer will always justify a higher price if he sees what he likes. As they say, "Buyers are liars." Eighty percent of all sales happen at a higher price than the customer swore he would pay.

❑ *Ask them not to buy.*
Suggesting that a new customer simply "look and get educated" on the first date makes them trust you and want to buy it even more.

❑ *Let them* **compare.**
Customers need to compare before buying. When they begin to shop, it's your best opportunity to show a wide range of product and s-t-r-e-t-c-h their budget.

❑ *Don't sell the wrong product.*
If the customer asks for a garage, don't show a carport. A salesperson's job is to *see* what customers like, not *tell* them what to like.

❑ *Get feedback.*
Ask your customers to tell you what they like and dislike about everything you show them. Their feedback will show you the way to close the sale.

❑ *Forewarn the buyer about "buyer's remorse."*
Soon after they say yes, most buyers believe their decision was wrong. Telling them about "buyer's remorse" then is too late. Telling them beforehand will keep their fear in check.

CUSTOMERS

❏ *Ask for the order and then* **shut up***!*
The silence might seem deafening to you, but it's not for buyers, because they can end it anytime.

❏ *Never expect loyalty.*
You'll have to earn it by building the customer's trust.

❏ *Don't waste time with the bottom fishers.*
They'll all still be waiting at the bottom same time next year.

PART 6
How to Prepare, Present, and Proceed with the Sales Presentation

Ask yourself this question: "If you were buying your product, would you buy it from you?" To become truly great in sales, you must genuinely believe *it's best* for the customer to buy the product from *you*!

Checklist for making great sales presentations

❏ *Practice makes perfect. Practice.*
Just as a performer never shows up on opening night without a dress rehearsal, you should never practice your sales presentation on a customer. Role-playing puts your inhibitions to rest and results in a well-prepared, confident delivery every time.

❏ *Ask to be last in line.*
When you know you'll be competing in a beauty lineup, ask for the last position. You don't want to hear "We still have a few other people to meet . . ." after you've made your sales presentation. If you're in the last position, your competitors are out of the way.

❏ *Make sure you have the customer's full attention.*
A distracted customer won't become a buyer.

❏ *Give yourself a title.*
The right title conveys power in the *customer's* mind, not in yours.

❏ *Put together an "I love me!" package.*
Create your own bragging book and fill it with your professional accomplishments, customer endorsements, and any press coverage you may have received. Be sure to include a detailed biography and a list of any school, club, or charity activities that you and your family participate in. Don't be shy, as customers fall for badges and endorsements. Size matters. Pull out all the stops and trumpet each success in the brightest color and largest typeface available. Our best salespeople's "I love me!" packages weigh in at more than five pounds.

❏ *Use third-party endorsements.*
Ask for and bring letters of recommendation from past customers. Potential customers like to see proof of your success, and are more comfortable saying yes in a crowd of happy customers.

❏ *If you don't have it, flaunt it anyway.*
Borrow your company's accomplishments and position them as "what we can do for you."

❏ *Make yourself half of a two-person sales team.*
Having a sales partner improves your confidence tenfold, and the attention of *two* salespeople is irresistible to most customers.

❏ *Take your assistant along.*
Customers respond well to someone important enough to have an assistant.

❏ *Show your enthusiasm!*
Customer surveys consistently show that enthusiasm is the

number one reason *why* customers bought from a particular salesperson. The number two reason is knowledge.

❏ *Always send a thank-you note, whether you won the business or not.*
Thank-you notes and customer guilt lead to future business. The best thank-you note is handwritten.

PRESENTING

PART 7
How to Communicate, Negotiate, and Close the Sale

Numbers don't kill deals, egos do. A salesperson's job is to control perception and keep everyone feeling like a winner. If one side feels that the other got the better deal, you can bet the deal will fall apart. A good deal is when each side is a little bit happy and a little bit sad. It's also the deal that sticks.

Checklist for negotiating the sale

❑ *Never take sides.*
   In negotiation, you need to stay independent so you can think independently.

❑ *Get all the facts before you start.*
   A small objection that is easily overcome soon becomes a nightmare when it's discovered too late in the negotiation.

❑ *Pinpoint each side's "hot button."*
   A successful negotiation is far more likely when you can figure out what's most important to each side.

❑ *Anticipate every possible objection.*
   It's the salesperson's responsibility to have an answer ready *before* a question is raised. A good sales exercise is to write down a commonly heard objection and then brainstorm every possible answer. Pick your best three and practice them until they roll off

your tongue. For example, when the customer says, "It's too expensive!" your response might be (a) "Yes, and it will only appreciate over time"; (b) "Yes, and everybody wants it"; (c) "Yes, and it has every feature you want"; (d) "Yes, and it has great tax advantages"; (e) "Yes, and can't you see yourself owning it?"; and, finally, (f) "Yes, and it's worth it!"

❏ *Don't carry messages, like a carrier pigeon.*
Instead, present them. Think of yourself as a prominent diplomat with a message that must be presented carefully. Instead of saying, "I have a low offer for you," try (a) "I have an excellent buyer, with impeccable credentials, and he's asked that I submit his offer of $X"; (b) "I'm happy to tell you I have an all-cash offer. It's somewhat less than what you're expecting, but the buyer is serious and he's willing to take delivery at your convenience"; or (c) "Today's your lucky day! I've got a real buyer on the hook, and he's asked that I submit an initial offer of $X."

❏ *Paint a happy picture.*
Always describe your customer as the "nice," "sincere," "fair" person he may or may not be.

❏ *Don't let the customer back himself into a corner.*
By not agreeing with his position, you give him the opening to later reverse his position and make his way out.

❏ *Don't rush the bid.*
Buyers change their mind when they are pushed to buy before they're really ready.

❏ *Don't ever suggest an opening bid.*
If you do, it quickly becomes the *new* asking price in the buyer's mind.

CLOSING

❏ *Dress up an offer by putting it in writing.*
Everyone takes a written offer more seriously.

❏ *Never refuse a low offer.*
Make a counterbid. Most deals start as low offers, and for some customers, it's a way to put their toe in the water.

❏ *Never submit your offer without a deadline.*
If there's no deadline for acceptance, a bid will often become the one to be bid against.

❏ *Never have the first bid accepted.*
People like to negotiate. When the buyer's first bid is accepted, the sale feels too easy and he'll almost always back out. Easy come, easy go.

❏ *Delay a quick counteroffer.*
When you reply "I'll try to have an answer for you in an hour" you build anticipation and give more credibility to what would have been a "too quick" response.

❏ *When you're expecting a low offer from a customer, forewarn the other side.*
An early heads-up is always appreciated. It leaves the door open and will soften the blow.

❏ *Avoid the Friday rush hour.*
People like to conclude business by the close of the business week. For example, in real estate, 80 percent of all offers are submitted on Fridays. Avoid the competition and push for a Thursday offer.

CLOSING

❏ *If your buyer gets cold feet, offer to show him more product.*
When the customer changes his mind about buying, take the pressure off by suggesting he see more product. It usually confirms his original decision.

❏ *Never go back empty-handed.*
Always get a counteroffer, no matter how small the concession. Going back without one is the equivalent of slamming the door in a suitor's face.

❏ *Whenever you're uncertain,* do nothing.
It's on the firing line that you're most apt to make a strategic mistake. Since very few sales are lost by taking a few minutes to think, step back and think through what your next move ought to be. You'll have the general's perspective and a much better shot at making the sale.

❏ *In heated competition, get your customer to put his best foot forward.*
Small incremental bid increases will only drive the price higher and inevitably won't secure the deal.

❏ *To overbid another buyer, ask the seller, "what number will make this deal happen?"*
Without knowing the number, you're only shadowboxing.

❏ *If you're asked to submit a closed bid, make your offer an uneven number.*
Bidding wars are often won by a few dollars.

❏ *Share a story about "the fish that got away."*
You can create urgency by sharing a story about someone else who waited and lost.

❏ *Play your hand to its best advantage.*
Price is not the only card in your hand. The other negotiating points are delivery date, financing terms, warranties, and extras.

❏ *Never leave only* **one** *remaining issue on the table.*
With only one question left to be resolved, there *has* to be a winner and a loser.

❏ *Get it in writing.*
Kisses aren't contracts.

PART 8
How to Jump a Slump

Sales is a business of fifteen noes to every one yes. Most sales slumps start when competition is stiff and one more lousy customer succeeds in wasting your time. You know you're headed for a slump when you start taking your business personally.

Steps for Getting Out of a Slump

1. Stop worrying about the next deal.
Instead, make weekly appointment goals and write them in your calendar. It'll take the pressure off and lay the right foundation for future sales.

2. Knock that chip off your shoulder.
It's a sure sign you're taking the business too personally.

3. Don't worry about what everybody else is thinking about you.
Nobody's watching and nobody gives a damn.

4. Make a plan of action.
Failure is a state of mind, but success is a state of action.

5. Mind your own business.

Stop comparing yourself to everybody around you. If you're minding someone else's business, who's minding yours?

6. Take a vacation.

Vacations are the best way to recharge your soul. Put aside the days for your next vacation now, and the one after that, too. Slumps never follow vacations.

Steps for Avoiding the Next Slump

1. Don't go to pity parties.

There can't be a pity party without two people. "Oh, poor me!" needs an "Oh, poor you." Stay away from complainers; they enable you to fail.

2. Stop watching the next guy.

You can't keep your eye on yourself and the next guy at the same time. It's just not true that everyone's making sales but you.

3. Don't try to sharp-shoot.

While you're being picky about what you're being picky about, your competitor is out with your customer. Sharp-shooting is the sales equivalent of throwing the dice and expecting to win every time.

4. Stop putting it off.

Procrastination is poisonous to success. Procrastination breeds guilt, guilt breeds depression, and depression breeds failure.

Best of luck

Barbara

Whatever Happened To . . .

(in order of appearance)

★ *. . . Mom & Dad?*
Florence and Ed live retired in Florida and live in a new four
bedroom, three bath beachfront condominium. Dad relaxes in
his La-Z-Boy watching his big screen TV, while Mom washes
beach towels for her visiting twenty-three grandchildren.

★ *. . . Ramòne Simòne?*
Ray and Tina remain happily married, have three children, and
live in suburban New York. The Pogue-Simone Company closed
in the early 1980s.

★ *. . . Gloria and the Fort Lee Diner?*
Gloria bought herself a pink Cadillac Eldorado and retired with
her two well-rounded friends to Virginia. The Fort Lee Diner is
now the Magic Wok Chinese Restaurant.

✷ ... *Palisade's Amusement Park?*

Irvin Rosenthal sold his amusement park and his stretch limo in the 1960s. The Caterpillar, the Giant Cyclone, and the world's largest salt water pool were replaced by 1200 condominium apartments.

✷ ... *Maggie O'Shay?*

Until her death in 1992, Mrs. O'Shay continued to pace up and down Undercliff Avenue minding everyone else's business. People regularly report sightings of her still inspecting Edgewater's lovely front yards.

✷ ... *John Campagna?*

My first landlord sold his apartment building and moved to Arizona. He e-mailed me after this book was published to say, "It wasn't my idea to evict you, it was the super's, Charlie O'Rourke!"

✷ ... *Sister Stella Marie?*

Sister terrorized the Holy Rosary School until 1962 when she left Edgewater. She died in 1994 and is buried at Holy Cross Cemetery in North Arlington, New Jersey. May she rest in peace.

✷ ... *Esther Kaplan?*

Esther retired as the president of The Corcoran Group in 2001. Esther is wealthy, lives in New York City with her husband and teaches adults how to read in her spare time. She still carries the most organized purse in town.

✷ ... *Bill Higgins?*

After years of counseling, Bill and I are happily married. Bill dabbled with teaching math and science in a Bronx elementary school, causing his knees to be replaced. He's now coaching our son in Little League baseball.

✶　*. . . Dad's Blue Beauty?* ·

Denise learned how to drive in Dad's prized Chevy station wagon, slamming the back end into the window of the Hackensack Bridal Shop and forcing Dad to buy fourteen bridal gowns. Next, Eddie learned to drive in Dad's dented Chevy station wagon, demolishing the front end by driving it through the plate glass window of Hiram's Hotdog Stand in Fort Lee.

✶　*. . . Ron Rossi?*

Ron skated his way to great sales success and landed The Corcoran Group's first million dollar listing in 1980. He was the first person we lost to the AIDS epidemic and his style and fun-loving spirit are still missed.

✶　*. . . Charlie's Boat?*

Charlie, the old Swede, took down the old shed in 1961, towed his sailboat to the Edgewater Marina, and sailed away.

✶　*. . . The Donald?*

After his failed bid for President of the United States, the Donald and his puffed blond helmet have moved on to a new career in television and movies.

✶　*. . . Carrie Chiang?*

Selling more than $100 million in real estate every year, Carrie holds her title as New York City's top condominium broker. Carrie still calls me "Baa-bwa."

✶　*. . . Chicky Dayock?*

The elegant Mrs. Dayock resides in Edgewater and directs its young citizens as the elementary school's crossing guard. Her daughter is married to the chief of police.

✭ *. . . Richard Seltzer, Esq.?*

After Richard whipped The Donald and collected our commission, he was promoted to senior partner at New York's Kaye Scholer LLP law firm. Richard is still beating bullies as the city's top litigator.

✭ *. . . #418 Undercliff Avenue?*

The Corcoran House was sold in 1978 and is again occupied by three families. The retaining wall is still there, Marty's pool is gone, and the rocks are no longer white.

Credits

Barbara's Heroic Mom
Florence Corcoran
Barbara's Loving Dad
Edwin Corcoran
Barbara's Leading Man
Bill Higgins
Barbara's Business Partner
Esther Kaplan
Barbara's Literary Agent
Stuart Krichevsky
Bruce's Co-Star
Scott Stewart
Bruce's Guardian Angel
Raymond Papa Littlefield
Bruce's Literary Agent
Mitchell Waters
Inspirational Teachers
Carolyn Randolph
Sandra Salinas
David Wertz

Key Players
Scott Durkin
Tresa Hall
Lori Levin
Sheryl Martinelli
Anita Perrone
Bob Sauer
Rebecca Wood
Secret Counsel
Sylvia Alpert
Ellen Carlson
Mary Cleary
Jennifer Mitchell
Imogene Mullin
Sy Presten
Joanne Rooney
RonDeena Ross
Liz Garland Sauer
Jennifer Stewart
Karen Williams

❋ ❋ ❋

President, Penguin Putnam
Susan Petersen Kennedy
Publisher and Editor, Portfolio
Adrian Zackheim
Director of Marketing, Portfolio
Will Weisser
Art Director
Joseph Perez
Publicist
Southerlyn Reisig
Associate Publicist, Portfolio
Allison Sweet

Illustrator
John Segal
Special Editor
Hilary Hinzmann
Special Art Director
Domenick Lorelli
Audio Director
Alisa Weberman
Production Editor
Kate Griggs
Editorial Assistant
Mark Ippoliti

And thank you to the incredible people of The Corcoran Group:

Guy Abernathy
Abdulraheem Abdul-
 muid
Jessica-Wind Abolafia
Robin Abramovitz
Melody Acevedo
Douglas Adams
Joan Adams
Karen Adler
Randy Aivazis
Douglas Albert
Griselle Aldarondo
John Alexopoulos
Mercedes Alvarez
Anthony Amato
Vera Amaya
Denise Andereya
Shavon Anderson
Franklin Angeles
Frederick Angeles
Haruno Arai
Jesse Archer
Tania Arias
David Arnold
Amy J. Arpadi
Ann Arthur
Ellen Arthur
Donald Artig
Antonio Astacio
Nicholas Athanail
Alisson Attwood
Beth Avery
Robert Aviles
Brian Babst
Brett Baccus
Wanda Bailey
Andrew Balaschak
Victoria Banks
Iona Baratz
Roseann Barber
Caryl Barnes
Pamela Barnes-Moses

Jeff Barnett
Enma Baron
Bo Bartlett
Lindsay Barton
Debbie Baum
Elissa Baum
Mark Baum
Sharon Baum
Michele Beaulieu
Henry R. Beck
Dee Dee Beckhorn
Gabriel Bedoya
Bill Begert
David Behin
Alexandra Bellak
Arthur Bellucci
Pamela Belsky
Joanne Benedict
Jeremy Bennett
Michael Bennett
Lara Berdine
Alan Berger
Carolyn Berger
Marjory Berkowitz
Adrienne Berman
Elise Berman
Cindy Bernat
Richard Bernstein
Antonella Bertello
Dolores Betsill
Froso Beys
Isabel Biderman
Ruth Bienstock
Joan Billick
Billy Billitzer
Anita Black
Sean Black
Marissa Blair
Patrick Blakslee
Cathy Blau
Shelly Bleier
Sage Blinderman

Arlyne Blitz
Kenny Blumstein
Meris Blumstein
Juanita Bobbitt
Kay Boecker
Alexis Bogen
Erin Boisson Aries
Kari Bolam
Julianne Bond
Sarah Bond
Joseph Bongiovanni
Andrew Booth
Suzanne Borowicz
Ruthann Bowers
Deanna Bowman
Eva Marie Bozsik
Jim Brawders
Cindy Breedy
Karesa Bridges
Elizabeth Bright
Jesus Brillembourg
Laura Brillembourg-
 Osio
Barbara Brine
Barton Brooks
Christina Brooks-
 Terrell
Marcia Browin-Irvin
Alysande Brown
Brad Brown
Caroline Brown
Garret Brown
Juliana Brown
Katie Brown
Lynne Brown
Robbie Brown
Tony Brown
Elizabeth Brownback
Irena Brownstein
Jay Brownstein
Gary Brynes
Fern Budow

Angela Buglisi
Karen Burden
Frances Burgarella
Laura Burkell
Sharon Burroughs-
Clarke
Paul Burton
Paula Busch
Anne Butler
Marianne Bye-
Miller
Sofiya Cabalquinto
Judy Cacase
Julia Cahill
Susan Caldwell
Tatiana Cames
Lisa Camilieri
Camille Campbell
Barry Campmier
Tonya Canady
Leighton Candler
Diane Cane
Nancy Capasso
Patricia Carbon
Enid Card
Fabio Carli
Loy Carlos
Cathleen Carmody
Barbara Casey
Karen Casey
Leslie Casey
Danielle Cash
Denise Castagna
Eric Castaldo
Anthony Castellano
Denise Cataudella
Benjamin Caushaj
Jennifer Cella
Rosemarie Ceraso
Catherine Certa
Suzanna Chan
Barbara Chase
Ella Chavers
Marisa Chaves

Tracy Chazin
Linda Chen
Debra Cheren
Carrie Chiang
Linda Chipurnoi
Eun Choi
Matthew Chook
Suan Chow
Sonia Christian
Eun Young Chung
Eric Ciambra
Jane Cibener
Lenny Cicio
Steve Cid
Victor Cino
Mark Ciolli
Peri Clark
Wendy Clark
Amanda Clarke
Tyrone Clerk
Patricia Cliff Warburg
Carol Cohen
Ingrid Cohen
Steven Cohen
Kelly Cole
Tricia Cole
Michael Coleman
Sharon Collington
Sheri Collins
Susanne Columbia
Peter Comitini
Lawrence Comroe
Carmen Cook
Jenifer Cook
Jody Cooney
Susan Cooper
Keith Copley
Daniel Cordeiro
James Cornell
Donald Correia
Antonio Cosentino
William Costigan
Mary Anne Cotter
Celine Coudert

Treadwell Covington
Debby Craker
Roger Creer
Joann Creighton
Victoria Crompton
Peter Cronin
Bill Cunningham
Syndi Cunto
Alain Da Sylveira
Andrea D'amico
David Daniels
Luke Danziger
Eric David
Brooke Davida
Penny Davidson
Eric Davis
Frances Davis
Ken Davis
Mona Davis
Nina De Rovira
Jodi De Vita
Elaine Dean
Heide Dechter
Brenda Decoursey
David Del Monte
Elena Del Valle
Paulette Demers
Alanna Dempewolff-
Barrett
Allan Dennis
Linda Derector
Nancy Derene-Seltzer
Mimi Derti
Thomas Di Domenico
Marisa Dichne
Carlos Diez
Kathleen Dillon
Connie Dingle
David Disick
Max Dobens
Jeffrey Doder
Janet Doerrer
Dennis Dolphin
Michael Dominick

Judah Domke
Jerry Dong
Jennifer Dorfmann
Coco Dorneanu
Roxana Dorneanu
Jackie Douek
Daniel Douglas
Joanne Douglas
Jonathan Douglas
Margaretta Douglas
Dee Downing
Ann Doyle
Judi Drogin
Elizabeth Duchardt
Siobhan Duffy
Patricia Dugan
Leslie Dumont
Karen Duncan
Stephen Dunn
Diane C. Dunne
Scott Durkin
Joseph Dwyer
Chisa Edwards
John Edwards
Dana Eggert
Tina Eichenholz
William Eichman
Amir El Moody
Adrian Ellias
Dare Elliott
Ingrid Ellis
Terrell Ellis
Eleanor Ellix
Viviane El-Yachar
David Enloe
Diane Erickson
Mary Ellen Erikson
Terry Erpenbach
Amanda Espinosa
Luke Evans
Mady Faber
Theresa Falgares
Andrew Farber
Edna Fast

Beverly Feingold
Dennis Feldman
Peter Feldman
Marcy Feltman
Amalia Ferrante
Angela Ferrante
Beth Ferrante
Amie Fields
Bruce Fields
Samarrah Fine
Jayne Firtell
Louise Fitting
Thomas Fitzpatrick
Sheila Flatley
Betsy Flynn
Linda Fonseca
Karen Fontana
Jacqueline Fopiano
Frank Ford
Brett Forman
Renee Forman
Sheba Forrest
Mary Fortuna
Joan Fox
Eileen Foy
Carmen Franco
Simone Franco
Steve Frank
Robyn Frank-Pedersen
Barbara Freehill
Ellen Freeman
Patrice Freeman
Inna Frenkel
Lorraine Friedberg
Marianna Friedman
Steve Friedman
Martha Friedricks
Charles Fritschler
Stacey Froelich
Alexandre Froes
Wigder Frota
Caroline Fuchs
Cathy Fuerth
Stephanie Gaasterland

Angelia Gabry
Patricia Galante
Jeffrey Gallo
Jennifer Garabedian
Martha Garcia
Camille Garelik
Nathan Garner
Louis Garrett
Greg Garwood
John Gasdaska
Carol Gat
James Gates
Erin Gaudreau
Maura Geils
Thomas Geisler
Heidi Geistwhite
Sara Gelbard
Alexandra George
Elizabeth Geraghty
Lynne Geras
Stan Gerasimczyk
Steven Gerber
Gerald Germany
Adi Gershoni
Linda Gertler
Aria Giauque
Heloisa Gilbert
Laurel Gilbride
Elizabeth J. Giles
Louisa Gillen
Justine Gilles
Judith Gilsten
Arden Ginsberg
Barry Giske
Paul Glenn
David Glick
Susyn Gliedman
Caroline Gold
Lisa Gold
Judyth Goldberg
Amy Goldberger
Maureen Goldstein
Mort Goldstein
Bennett Goldworth

America Gonzalez
Isabel Gonzalez
Lisa Gonzalez
Barbara Goodman
Marc J. Goodman
Linda Gorby
Julie Gordon
Michael Gordon
Anne Gorey
Damon Gorton
Barbara (Clement)
  Gould
Richard Gould
Robbie Gould
Dolores Grant
Adrienne Gratry
Dava Grayson
Joseph Grayson
Christine Graziano
Bob Green
Crystal Green
Irsa Greene
Judith Greene
Lori Greene
Rhonda Greenwald
Dorothy Greiner
Karesse Grenier
Daniel Grey
Jim Gricar
Rose Grobman
Alison Gross
Lili Gross
Deborah Grubman
Marianne Guadiana
Helen Guittard
Elyse Gutman
Joseph Guzzo
Suzanne Halasz
Gregory Hall
Tresa Hall
Susan Halpern
Timothy Hamm
Joy Handler
Kathie Hannaford

Donald Hannibal
Elizabeth Harding
Judith Harrison
Christine Harste
Marsha Hartstein
Atoussa Haskin
Meredith Hatfield
Nicole Hatoun
Steven R. Hauser
Dean Hawthorne
Benjamin Hayden
Julie Hayek
James Hayes
Kevin Hayes
Nisha Hayes
Harriet Haynes
Zachary Haynes
Carole Healy
Suzanne Hebron
Margaret Heffernan
Sharon Held
Barbara Heller
Yvonne Hemming
Diane Henning
Jacqueline Henriquez
Eric Heras
Terry Herbert
Katrina Hering
David Hertz
Barbara Hochhauser
Debra Hoffman
Eileen Hoffman
Susan Holden
Carol Holder
Deborah Hollon
Yury Holohan
Hilary Holt
Linda Homler-Ferber
Linda Honan
Hillary Hopkins
John Hopkins
Jennifer Hoxter
Lily Hu
Robin Hudis

Caitlin Hughes
Dennis R. Hughes
Taryn Hughes
Holly Hunt
Danny Huynh
Eli Ickovic
Dorian Irizarry
Debbie Isaacs
Christine Iu
Carol Jacobanis
Alton James
Steven James
Carla Jean
Deirdre Jennette
Brian Johnson
Ingrid Johnson
Michael Johnson
Susan Johnson
Heather Johnson-
  Sargent
Allison Jones
Michael Jones
Sharon Jordan
Bo Jung
Jacqueline Kabat
Joyce Kafati-Batarse
Gary Kahn
Greg Kammerer
Christopher Kann
Joan Kaplan
Rachel Kaplan
Marcia Kapp
Jason Karadus
Bill Karam
Carey Karmel
Karron Karr
Kara Kasper
Masanori Katagiri
Howard Katz
Sharon Katzoff
Claire Kaufman
Debra Kavaler
Renee Kaye
Darren Kearns

Judy Kekesi
Lynn Kellert
Carol Kelly
Frank Kelly
Meghan Kelly
Beth Kenkel
Shawna Kent
Sarah Kerzner
Cynthia Keskinkaya
Anne Kettle
James Kim
Kyeong-Soo Kim
Lynn Kim
Dannie King
Grant King
Warren King
Lucy Kirk
Naomi Klein
Jan Kline
Rebecca Knaster
Jennifer Knestrick
Jack Koenig
Larisa Kogut
Karen Kohen
Jana Kolpen
Jennifer Konsevitch
Anna Kopel
Svetlana Kopil
Amir Korangy
Jussara Korngold
Victoria Kortes
Deanna Kory
Jane Koryn
Gale Kotlikova
Marianna Kotlyar
Ellen Kourtides
Olya Kovacevic
Ildi Kovacs
Bill Kowalczuk
Andrew Kramer
Highlyann Krasnow
Robert Krieger
Peter Krimstock
Ralph Krueger

Dmitry Kruglov
Irene Kruglova
Matthew Kuriloff
Emily Kwok
Charles Laboz
Debra Lachance
Jaswant Lalwant
Stephanie Lambrecht
Douglas Lamere
Jody Lamonte
Eileen Lamorte
Dorothy Langan
Eileen Langer
Shirley Langworthy
Joseph Lapiana
Rose Marie Laster
Inge Lasusa
Lorraine Latchman
Maria Latchman
Mitzie Lau
Steven Laurelli
Ellie Lavi
Kristi Law
Comroe Lawrence
Marc Lawrence
Mitchell Lawrence
Rand Lawrence
Tracy Lawrence-
   Brookman
Magalie Lazarus
Christopher Leavitt
Fabienne Lecole
Betty Lee
Jennifer Lee
Nancy Lee
Susan Lee
Martine Lefebvre
Richard Leitner
Susanna Lendrum
Adam Leon
Ellen Leon
Denise Leonetti-
   Kynman
Nora Leonhardt

Thomas Leung
Isabella Levenson
Lori Levin
Abby Levine
Neil Levine
Jeff Levitas
Susan Levy
Jacqueline Lew
David Lewandowski
Cecilia Li
Nina Liebman
Pam Liebman
Deborah Liebman-
   Bernstein
Peter Lione
Rena Lipiner
Rebecca Lippiner
Lisa Lippman
Kedakai Lipton
Carolyn Little
Fran Litwack
Charles Lobel
Shelly Lobel
Alexandra Loeb
Rosalie Loew
Elliott Lokitz
Sheila Lokitz
Jennifer Loukedis
Nancy Love
Scarlett Lovell
Brian Lover
Courtney Loving
Irene Lowenkron
Janet Lowry
Beth Lowy
Thomas Lowy
Rodolfo Lucchese
Meredith Luck
Frances Lucy
Michael Lui
Jocelyn Lumbao
Vladimir Luzader
Robert N. Lynn
Nan Lyons

Maggie Macdonald
Clarissa Mack
Keith Mack
Matthew Mackay
Rodney Mackay
Rita Madan
Melinda Magnett
Charlotte Maier
Anna Makarova
Eliada Maldonado
Serena Maldonado
Elyse Mallin
Barrie Mandel
Joanna Mandel
Zoe Mandel
Dennis Mangone
Jill Mangone
Jean (Gigi) Mankoff
Eileen Mann
Francesca Mannarino
Jean Manon
Susan Mansell
Maria Manuche-Allen
Bob Manzari
Steven Manzi
David Marangio
Maritza Marcano
Loretta Maresco
Nordine Marniche
Ivor Marryshow
Leslie Marshall
William Marshall
Ellen Martin
Jane Martin
Kerry Martin
William Martin
Sheryl Martinelli
Carmen Martinez
Gene Martinez
Peter Martino
Jennifer Marwood
Sherry Matays
James Mathieu
Keiko Matsumura

Barbara J. Matter
Dana Maurer
Tami Mayer
Kathy Ann Mazzola
Robert Mazzola
Maria Mazzuckis
Joan McArdle
Bonnie McCartney
Eileen McCauley
James McDade
Missy McDonald
Eric McFarland
Cindy McField
Cristina McGillicuddy
Laina McGowan
Valerie McKee
Madeline McKenna
Joan McLaughlin
Kyle McLaughlin
Deborah McLoughlin
Marta McLoughlin
Dan McNally
Mary Jo McNally
Brian McQuade
Spencer Means
Jill Meilus
Rachel Melniker
Felix Melo
David Menendez
Julia Menocal
Lolis Merope
Betsy Messerschmitt
Lisa Meyer
Lisa H. Meyer
Mary Micali
Jean Michael
Jeanne Michels
Scott R. Michener
Laura Denise
    Milkowski
Brandon Miller
Liane Miller
Michael Mills
Willard Mills III

Rodney Mims
Jerry Minsky
Eileen Mintz
Armando Miranda
Rebecca Mirkin
Michael Misisco
Michelle Mizrahi
Anna Moll Moers
Colleen Mohan
Monique Mohan
Juan Moldes
David Molk
Pablo Montes
Frosty Montgomery
Kenneth Moore
Scott Moore
Millie Morales
Michael S. Moran
Christine Morgan
Debra A. Morgan
Ellen Morgan
Gayle Morgan
Anthony Morris
Brian Morris
Shirley Morris
Kate Morton
Stuart Moss
Susan Moss
Jennifer Motisi
Elizabeth Mottram
Danny Mui
John Muir
Connie Mui-Reilly
Kathy Mulkeen
Jorge Murillo
Mimi Murphy
Loring Murtha
Lauren Muss
Sara Narins
Joshua Nathanson
Vicki Negron
Kelly Neinast
Patricia Neinast
Bettina Nelson

George Nelson
Cheryl Nesbit
Dalia Newman
Ellen Newman
Molly Newman
Latenya Newton
Alex Nicholas
Roseann Nielsen
Cheryl Nielsen-Saaf
Rodney Nixon
Michael Nolan
Peter Noonan
Paula Novick
Maria Novo
Tony Oakley
Daniel O'Connell
Carol O'Connor
Kay O'Connor
Kristina Ojdanic
Erica Ojeda
Shelley O'Keefe
Charles Olson
Ezra Orchard
Michael O'Reilly
Shuli Orgad
Albert Orlick
Melissa Osterhart
Judy Oston
Emilie O'Sullivan
Jessica Ott
Julie Owen
Nina Owens
Leah Ozeri
Adam Pacelli
Elan Padeh
Harjit (Tony) Pahuja
Pat Palermo
Adelaida Palm
Dorian Palumbo
Michael Pangalos
Sandra Papale
Matt Parrella
Linda Partland
Maria Pashby

Faruk Pasic
Alok Patel
Ketul Patel
Nrupal Patel
Pinkal Patel
Robert Paterson
Maria Paula
Georgine Paulin
Jeffrey Peckage
Sandra Pedraza
Lois Peerce
Frank Percesepe
Carmen Perez
Yolanda Perez
Melinda Perkins
Steve Perlo
Anita Perrone
Christian Perry
Lione Peter
Rasheeda Peterson
Brandon Phay
Laurie Phelan
Nina Phillips
R. Brian Philpott
Jason Phoel
Dominique Pickens
Marc Pignitor
Alexander Pisa
Elizabeth Pisanchik
Deirdre Poe
Johanna L. Politzer
Joseph Polivy
Johanna Poltzer
Christine Ponz
Susan Postman
Patricia Powell
Christian Powers
Joanna M. Prettitore
Anne Prosser
Allison Pulito
Deborah Puza-Jensen
Tiesha Quinones
Melissa Quintana
Jackie Ramirez

Eric Ramme
Kim Rand
Robert Rankin
Neeri Rao
Angela Rapoport
Elaine Raskind-Evons
Karen Rasmussen
Steen Rasmussen
Karin Rathje-
    Posthuma
Marlys Ray
Diana Rayzman
Shannon Reese
Ahmed Rehan
Alison Reiser
Southerlyn Reisig
Samantha Reiss
Alfred Renna
Shlomi Reuveni
Brian Rice
Denice Rich
Roy Richards
Rodney Richardson
Jason Riggs
James Rigney
Monica Rittersporn
Nadine Robbins
Adam Roberts
Lisa Roberts
Natella Rocca
Alan Roditi
Ana Rodriguez
Grace Rodriguez
Erin M. Roe
Tracey Rogers
Michael Rohrer
Reyna Rojas
Rick Rome
Cc Rose
Julie Rosenblatt
Jim A. Rosenbloom
Layla Rosenfeld
Beth Ross
Wendy Rosset

Beverley Rouse
Andre Rozzell
Alida Rubin
Dell Rubin
Jayne Rubin
Josh Rubin
Barry Rudnick
Elizabeth Rueckerl-
  Betteil
Gale Rundquist
Leslie Rupert
Charles Russell
Shelly Russell
Ronnie Russo-
  Landau
Steven Rutter
Maureen Ryan
Deborah Sabec
Joshua Sachs
Barbara Sagan
Marcy Sakhai
Sherry Sakoor
Anne Marie Salmeri
Marcia Salonger
Vicki Salsberg
Edith Salton
Carol Samaras
Ruth Samuels
Athena Sanchez
Pamela Sanders
Alan Sands
Alba Sanjurjo
Maria Santander
Daria Saraf
Wendy Sarasohn
Ralph Sassone
Sandra Sautner
Kerri-Anne Scalia
Howard Schein
Kathleen Scheerle
Lawrence Schier
Glenn Schiller
Linda Schlang
Daniella G. Schlisser

Barbara A. Schmidlin
Marie Schmon
Deborah Schneider
Hallie Schneider
Mark Schoenfeld
Christine Scholtz
Lara Schultz
Barbara Schwartz
John Schwartz
Peter Schwartz
Sheryl Schwartz
Jackie Schwimmer
Elizabeth
  Scordamaglia
Timothy Scott
Jennifer Seda
John Segal
Spencer Seid
Scott Seisler
Sally Semrad
Jerry Senter
Pat Serby Hoxter
Michael Serman
Sara Settembrini
Adriana Sforza
Carol Shainswit
Katja Shamburger
Ryan Shane
James Shao
Tami Shaoul
Sharone Shatz
Nicole Shaw
Sandy Shaw
Jill Sherwood
Chandra Shiwsanker
Vidya Shiwsanker
Jeff Sholeen
Michael Shulman
Monique Silberman
Vanessa Silberman
Janet Silva
Richard Silver
Dana Simonetti
Dee Simonson

Amy Singer
Shirley Singer
Susan Singer
Leigh Sioris
Eddie Siso
Kathy Slattery
Adam Slocum
Deborah Small-
  Kornfeld
Barbara F. Smith
Jeffrey A. Smith
Lindsay Smith
Lisa Smith
Michael Smith
Anne Snee
Pat Snell
Tina Soares
Jenifer Sokoloff
Tami Soloman
Kitty Sorell
Melissa Sosa
Keilani Soto
Kim Soule
Elizabeth Spahr
Emily Spahr
Lynn Spanich
Fred Specht
Angelo Spells
Linda Spencer
Shari Sperling
Howard Spiegelman
Richelle Spindell
William Spiros
Heather Spirtos
Sarit Spivak-Svelitsky
Maryann Squires
Tim Standard
Wendy Stark
John Stathis
Rhea Stein
Marlene Steiner
William Stephen
Susanne Steward
Barbara Stewart

Scott Stewart
Linda Stillwell
Minette Stokes
Taryn Stowe
Lisa Sulfaro
Gregory Sullivan
Martha Sussman
Katsuko Suzuki
Rebecca Swanner
Ric Swezey
James Swimm
Ellen Sykes
Michael Sykes
Soho Tada
Dia Tam-Suzuki
Catherrine Tarkas
Alice Taussig
Carol M. Taxon
Nancy Teague
Jacky Teplitzky-
  Dobens
Victoria Terri-Cote
Thomas Tevana
Sarah Thanhauser
Lovelyn Thevenin
Terence Thomas
Kai Thompson
Lois Thompson
Sharon Thompson
Angelica Thompson
  Ruiz
Clare Timoney
Donna Tirella
Gregory Todd
Christopher Tomaino
Dolores Tomaino
Ruth Tomeck
Pam Tomlin
Frank Torre
Carlos Torres
Lolly Totero
Cay Trigg
Carolyn Trilli
Laurie Trontz

Matt Tsopanidis
Suzanne Turkewitz
Karen Tutty
April Tyler
Elizabeth Ughetta
Stacia Upham
Nancy Van
  Bourgondien
Dale Van Dyke
Nelly Van Kooy
Anneke Van Wagoner-
  Felske
Stephanie
  Vandenwallbak
Luz Vargas
Helen Varvarides
Lennie Varvarides
Margaret Velard
Maxime Velard
Jacqueline Vincent
Rosalie Vinci
Karl Von Freiling
Eric Von Kuersteiner
Cindy Wachter
Elizabeth Wainstock
Sara Waisman
Carolyn Waldman
Ginny Waldman
Maria Wall
Maria Wallace
Janet Wang
Peter Warnke
Elizabeth Warshaw
Kim Waters
H. Barry Wayne
Gloria Weber
William Wedell
Janet Weiner
Joy Weiner
Jordan Weiss
Arlene Weissberg
Joyce Weisshappel
Jenifer Werblow
Diane Weston

Rebecca Wetzler
Paul Wexler
Thomas Wexler
Jarrett White
Patricia Whitehead
Rose-Marie Whitelaw
Cindy Whiteside
Justin Whitney
Frances Wholey
Carter Wilcox
Magillia Wilford
Amani Willett
Anthony Williams
Grace Williams
Jason Williams
Katie Williams
Neoly Lika Williams
Sarah Williams
Jane Wilson
Nellie Wilson
Sandy Wilson
Vie Wilson
Arleen Winick
Gabriella Winter
Marc Wisotsky
Catherine Witherwax
Suzanne Wolf
Linda Wolff
Kathy Wong
Meredith (Phooi)
  Wong
Thomas Wong
Marlena Wood
Erin Woodward
Pam Wright
Sheila Wyle
Jack Xue
Mike Yablon
Arina Yakobi
Julie Yakov
Rumi Yasuda
Dina Yoel
Dianne Young
Harold Young

Leah Young
Pamela Young
Susan Zabatta
Rosemarie Zanghellini
Lauren Zehner

Dorothy Zeidman
Nela Zelensky
Ivona Zeler
Lee Zimmerman
Melissa Ziweslin

Eric Zollinger
Paul Zumoff
Eva Zurek

And thank you to our new parents at The Corcoran Group:

Henry R. Silverman
Richard Smith
Bob Becker

Index